# Maya Mythology

*Captivating Maya Myths of Gods, Goddesses and Legendary Creatures*

# Free Bonus from Captivating History
# (Available for a Limited time)

Hi History Lovers!

Now you have a chance to join our exclusive history list so you can get your first history ebook for free as well as discounts and a potential to get more history books for free! Simply visit the link below to join.

Captivatinghistory.com/ebook

Also, make sure to follow us on:

Twitter: @Captivhistory

Facebook: Captivating History:@captivatinghistory

# Contents

# Introduction

The story of Maya culture extends in an arc that reaches back nearly four thousand years, with the first small settlements being established around 2000 BCE, through to the zenith of Maya civilization between about 250 and 900 CE, and ending with the gradual collapse of Maya cities beginning in the tenth century, which became complete with the Spanish incursions into southern Central America in the sixteenth and seventeenth centuries. Unlike their Aztec cousins to the north, the Maya were able to hold out against the Spanish until the late seventeenth century, and since that time have been more successful than their cousins at maintaining their languages, many of their traditional religious practices, and other important aspects of their culture, despite colonial rapacity and influences.

Unfortunately, the amount of information about ancient Maya myth and culture that still survives today is shockingly small. Under Spanish rule, all but four Maya codices were destroyed, and early Spanish historians and chroniclers such as Diego de Landa (1524-1579)—who as Bishop of Yucatan oversaw the burning of Maya books—declined to record Maya myths and other literary forms, although their writings do relate quite a bit about Maya culture, society, and religious practices.

What little Maya myth we have today is recorded in two sources: the *Popol Vuh*, the main book of K'iche' Maya myth; and the *Books of Chilam Balam*, which were compiled by Yucatec Maya redactors in the seventeenth and eighteenth centuries. The latter are named after the places where they were compiled (e.g. *Chilam Balam of Chumayel*; *Chilam Balam of Mani*).

The K'iche' are one of several branches of Maya culture. They took up residence in the highlands of what are now Guatemala and El Salvador after the fall of Chichen Itza, probably sometime in the early thirteenth century. Today, they live in Guatemala. The *Popol Vuh* continues to be a touchstone for the K'iche' of Guatemala today, as well as for other Maya peoples, and was declared the national book of Guatemala in 1971.

Compiled around 1550, the *Popol Vuh* is an important sacred text preserving ancient epic tales of the creation of the world, a mythical early history of the Maya people and their culture, and the adventures of Hunahpu and Xbalanque, the Hero Twins who overcome monsters and giants, play the sacred ballgame against the Lords of Death themselves, and eventually are transformed into the sun and moon.

*The Books of Chilam Balam* (Books of the Jaguar Priest) are written in a Yucatec Maya dialect, and reflect the culture and traditions of the Maya from the Yucatan Peninsula. There are nine extant *Books of Chilam Balam*, all of which were compiled in the seventeenth and eighteenth centuries by Maya redactors. The three most important of these are the books in Chumayel, Tzizimin, and Mani. While the *Popol Vuh* is a coherent set of epic myths, the *Chilam Balam* books are more miscellanies or commonplace books, containing varied collections of ancient myth, history, ritual, almanacs, and other information, including prophecies about the advent of the Spanish. Looking at the myths that the *Books of Chilam Balam* contain gives

2

us a hint of the variety of ancient Maya traditions and beliefs, as these Yucatec myths are substantially different from those preserved in the K'iche' *Popol Vuh.*

Although the Yucatec and K'iche' Maya traditions are different from one another, neither were isolated from other Mesoamerican cultures. For example, the K'iche' and Yucatec pantheons both include an analog of the Aztec Quetzalcoatl, the Plumed Serpent, who is called *Gucumatz* by the K'iche' and *Kukulcan* by the Yucatec Maya. However, while the Plumed Serpent functions as a creator god for the K'iche', he does not appear in the Yucatec creation myth at all.

Another point of contact with Aztec myth that differs between the K'iche' and Yucatec Maya is that the Yucatec creation myth conceptualizes the material of the earth as having been made out of the body of a crocodilian creature called *Itzam Cab Ain* (lit. "Iguana Earth Crocodile"), which recalls Aztec myths about Cipactli and Tlaltecuhtli, both of which were water-dwelling monsters who were turned into the earth by the gods. A monster such as this is entirely absent from the K'iche' tales of creation.

Myths from the Yucatec and K'iche' traditions make up the bulk of the tales presented in this book, which also contains other Maya folktales. The first section of this volume is devoted to creation myths, one from the *Popol Vuh* and the other from the *Books of Chilam Balam.* The second section relates the tales of Hunahpu and Xbalanque, the Hero Twins from the *Popol Vuh,* and the third section contains three traditional Maya folktales unrelated to either the *Popol Vuh* or the *Chilam Balam* sources.

Since many translators and editors of these stories tend to present the names of gods and other characters in English translation rather than the Maya original, I have maintained that convention here, with two exceptions: the first is in cases where accurate translations are not available, and the second is in the Yucatec creation myth, for reasons of prosody.

3

From the fantastic exploits of the Hero Twins, to the stories of how the world came to be, to folktales about people, animals, and supernatural beings, Maya myth presents us with a fascinating variety of characters, plots, and imagery. All of these tales, whether from an ancient or more modern source, show us the great richness and beauty of Maya literature.

## The Maya Calendar

For the Maya, as for other Mesoamerican peoples, accurate timekeeping was of paramount importance, primarily for agricultural and religious reasons. And similarly to other Mesoamerican cultures such as the Aztecs, the Maya kept both a 360-day solar calendar with five intercalary days tacked on to the end of the year and a 260-day ritual calendar.

The structure of the Maya calendar is nearly identical to the Aztec one. The 260-day ritual calendar is known as the Sacred Round and is often referred to by the Yucatec Maya term *Tzolk'in*, or *Chol Q'ij* in K'iche'. This calendar is comprised of an interlocking round of twenty sacred day names and thirteen day numbers. The day names are used in a recurring specified order, preceded by the day number. Each day is called by number and name, for example, 5 Ix or 11 Ahau. When the thirteenth day is reached, the count begins again with 1 on the next day name in the series. This produces a set of 260 unique day designations. Below is a table that gives an idea of how the number and day systems interact with one another.

## Table 1: The Sacred Round

*Translations of day names from Prudence M. Rice,* Maya Calendar Origins: Monuments, Myth History, and the Materialization of Time *(Austin: University of Texas Press, 2007), p. 34.*

The solar calendar is called *Haab'*, and consists of eighteen months of twenty days each, plus an additional five intercalary days at the end of the year. These five additional days are considered to be very unlucky.

| Day Name | Translation | Day Counts | | |
|----------|-------------|------|------|------|
| Imix | Water Lily | 1 | 8 | 2 |
| Ik | Wind | 2 | 9 | 3 |
| Akbal | Darkness | 3 | 10 | 4 |
| Kan | Yellow | 4 | 11 | 5 |
| Chicchan | Snake | 5 | 12 | 6 |
| Cimi | Death | 6 | 13 | 7 |
| Manik | Deer | 7 | 1 | 8 |
| Lamat | Venus | 8 | 2 | 9 |
| Muluc | Water | 9 | 3 | 10 |
| Oc | Foot | 10 | 4 | 11 |
| Chuen | Monkey | 11 | 5 | 12 |
| Eb | Tooth | 12 | 6 | 13 |
| Ben | Cane | 13 | 7 | 1 |
| Ix | Jaguar | 1 | 8 | 2 |
| Men | Eagle | 2 | 9 | 3 |
| Cib | Buzzard | 3 | 10 | 4 |
| Caban | Earth | 4 | 11 | 5 |

| Etznab | Flint | 5 | 12 | 6 |
| Cauac | Rain | 6 | 13 | 7 |
| Ahau | Lord | 7 | 1 | 8 *etc.* |

**Table 2: Haab' Month Names**

| Yucatecan Name | Translation |
| --- | --- |
| Pop | Mat |
| Wo | Frog |
| Sip | Stag |
| Sotz' | Bat |
| Sek | Skull |
| Xul | End |
| Yaxk'in | Green Day |
| Mol | Gather |
| Ch'en | Well |
| Yax | Green |
| Sak | White |
| Kej | Deer |
| Mak | Cover |
| K'ank'in | Yellow Day |
| Muwan | Owl |
| Pax | Drum |
| K'ayab' | Turtle |
| Kumk'u | Dark |
| Wayeb' | Specter |

*Wayeb' is the set of five unlucky days at the end of the year. All other months have twenty days.*

*After Prudence M. Rice,* Maya Calendar Origins: Monuments, Myth History, and the Materialization of Time *(Austin: University of Texas Press, 2007), p. 41.*

In addition to the 365 days of the solar calendar and the 260 days of the Sacred Count, the Maya recognized other important blocks of time. The chart below shows how the system builds up from a single day, or *k'in*, into larger and larger units up through the *b'ak'tun*. This reckoning of large units of time is known as the Maya Long Count.

**Table 3: The Long Count**

| Unit | Value | Number of Days | Approximate Gregorian Value |
|------|-------|----------------|-----------------------------|
| k'in | | 1 day | |
| winal | 20 k'in | 20 days | |
| tun | 18 winal | 360 days | 1 year |
| k'atun | 20 tuns | 7,200 days | 20 years |
| b'ak'tun | 20 k'atuns | 144,000 days | 396 years |

*Table compiled from information in Prudence M. Rice,* Maya Calendar Origins: Monuments, Myth History, and the Materialization of Time *(Austin: University of Texas Press, 2007), p. 44.*

# PART I: TWO CREATION MYTHS

### The Creation Tale from the *Popol Vuh*

*For the K'iche' Maya, creation did not happen in one fell swoop, but rather in stages. The gods make several failed attempts at creating people who might speak to and honor them before they finally arrive at beings that are complete, and they succeed only when they create the people out of maize, the most important Maya staple food. We also see in this story the central importance of speech and timekeeping to the Maya, since it is through speech that the gods wish to be honored and addressed, and since they wish the people to keep a sacred calendar so that they might know when to honor the gods. The Maya gods therefore are not infallible, nor are they entirely self-sufficient: they can make mistakes, and they require the attention and adoration of sentient beings for their own sustenance.*

In the beginning, there was nothing but sky and the waters beneath the sky. And the waters were still, the waters of the great sea of the beginning, but the sea was empty and void, and no creatures lived within it, there under the sky. There was no earth. There were no

9

fish, no birds, no animals, no people. All was water and sky, there alone in the dark.

But far down within the waters, down deep at the bottom of the bottomless sea, were Tepeu the Ruler and Gucumatz the Plumed Serpent. The Ruler and the Plumed Serpent were with the other Creators, The One Who Bears and The One Who Begets, and The One Who Makes and The One Who Molds. Together all these Creators were hidden at the bottom of the bottomless sea under a great many quetzal feathers and cotinga feathers, bright feathers of blue and of green, of black and ruby, and there only was light. And up high within the sky, high above the bottomless waters, was Heart of Sky. Heart of Sky was both one and three, and the three are Thunderbolt Hurricane, Youngest Hurricane, and Sudden Thunderbolt.

Heart of Sky sent their word to the Plumed Serpent, and together they spoke of the world. "The world is empty," they said. "How shall we fill it?"

Together Heart of Sky and the Plumed Serpent spoke of all the things they would make with Tepeu and the other Creators who lived at the bottom of the bottomless sea. They planned and they thought, they talked of the things they would make, of the plants and animals, and of the people. This happened because Heart of Sky sent their word to the Plumed Serpent; it was their word that began the beginning of things.

When all had been planned, when the shapes of all things had been decided and agreed upon, the Creators first moved aside the waters. They parted the sea, they emptied it out, they bent their thought to their creation and lo! the earth came into being. From the earth sprang mountains and hills, and on the mountains and hills were forests of green trees, and between the mountains and hills the creators let flow the rivers and the streams, and the waters of the sea surrounded the earth.

The Plumed Serpent looked upon the earth that was made and said, "Heart of Sky! This was a fine thought you had, to create new things. I am pleased with this earth."

Heart of Sky replied, "Yes, it is good. But still we must make the people, for without the people, there will be no one to thank us or praise us for what we have done and what we have yet to do."

And so, it was by the thoughts and words of the Creators that the earth came into being out of the waters of the sea, and the sky was set above the earth and the waters.

Next the Creators took counsel among themselves as to what manner of beasts and birds should live upon the earth. The One Who Bears and The One Who Begets said, "The world is silent. There only is earth, and water, and trees, and bushes. We should make guardians for these things."

And when they had said this, the deer and the birds came into being. The One Who Bears and The One Who Begets gave homes to the deer. They said to the deer, "Live in the forests and along the rivers. Go into the meadows. These places are to be your home, and there shall you bear your young. You will walk on all fours."

Next The One Who Bears and The One Who Begets gave homes to the birds. They said to the birds, "Live in the trees and the bushes; make your nests in them. There shall be your homes, and there shall you bear your young. You shall fly in the sky."

In this wise, the One Who Bears and The One Who Begets gave homes to the deer and the birds, to the jaguar and the serpents, to all the birds and all the beasts.

When that was done and all the creatures were in their proper places, The One Who Bears, The One Who Begets, The One Who Makes, and The One Who Molds said to them, "Speak! Talk to one another! Say our names to us, for we have created you. Pray to us, and keep sacred our holy days."

The jaguar heard the command of the Creators, but it did not say their names. It only roared. The birds heard the command of the Creators, but they did not say their names. They only sang their songs and called their calls. None of the birds or beasts was able to say the names at all, for they did not have languages to speak with.

"Oh!" cried the Creators. "Oh, this has gone badly. The birds and the beasts cannot say our names, even though it is we who have created them."

The Creators then said to the birds and the beasts, "From now on, the canyons and mountains shall be your homes. From now on, you shall provide a service, and that is that your flesh shall become food. This we ordain, for you failed to give us the proper honor that is our due; you did not say our names, and you cannot keep sacred our holy days."

And thus it was that the Creators made the birds and the beasts, and gave them homes, and thus it was that the flesh of the birds and the beasts became food, because they could not speak, but only make the sounds that belong to each kind of creature.

Again, the Creators took counsel among themselves about what to do. The One Who Makes and The One Who Molds spoke together with The One Who Bears and The One Who Begets. They said, "We must try again. The birds and the beasts cannot do for us what is needful. We must make a new creature, one that can speak, one that can keep sacred our holy days, one that can praise us and nurture us as we deserve."

So, the Creators took up some earth, they took up some mud. They patted it, they shaped it, they made it into a form of a body. No matter how they tried to shape it, it crumbled. The body crumbled, it became soft, it fell apart. They could not get the head set upon it in the correct way. It could not see properly. It spoke, but it had no understanding. And when it went into the water, it dissolved away, it flowed away with the current of the water.

The One Who Makes and The One Who Molds said, "This was not successful. The body we made was not strong enough. It could speak, but it dissolved too quickly in the water. It could not bear young. It could not keep holy our sacred days. We must try again."

And so, the Creators went to the other gods for aid. They went with Ruler and Heart of Sky and Plumed Serpent, to those who were seers and keepers of time and of days. They went to Xpiyacoc, who is Grandmother of Day. They went to Xmucane, who is Grandmother of Light. They went to Hunahpu Possum and Hunahpu Coyote. They called upon Great Peccary and Great Tapir. They called upon those who are Masters of their Art.

"Tell us," said the Creators. "Tell us how we might make beings to care for us and worship us. Cast maize and the seeds of the coral tree for divination. Tell us how it shall go if we make beings out of wood, for you are the ones who have the wisdom to see."

Xpiyacoc and Xmucane cast maize in divination. They cast the seeds of the coral tree. They worked their art of divination, and they said to Heart of Sky and the Plumed Serpent and to all the Creators, "Yes, your thought is good. Make new beings from wood. Make them so that they might speak and live."

The Creators said, "Let it be thus," and from those words creatures come into being, people made from wood. The One Who Makes made the man from the wood of the coral tree. The One Who Molds made the woman out of reeds. These creatures could walk, and talk, and bear young, and walk upon the earth, but because they were made of wood and reeds they had no souls, and their bodies were poorly fashioned and very dry. They did not know their Creators. They did not know Heart of Sky. They went about their daily business without thinking at all of those who had created them, without saying their names.

Heart of Sky therefore made a flood and a disaster to destroy the people made from wood. Heart of Sky sent a flood to wash them away, and the destroyers to destroy the people made from wood, to gouge out their eyes and cut off their heads, to eat them and to rend their bodies. This was done because the people made from wood did not give proper honor to those who had created them.

Hurakan came, the one who is a great storm. The rain fell and fell and fell, all day and all night. Beasts from the forests came into the houses of the wooden people. Their household belongings turned upon them, their dogs and turkeys turned upon them. Their household belongings rose up and beat them; they hit the man and the woman in their faces.

The dogs and turkeys said, "You ate us once, but now we shall eat you!"

The stone for grinding corn said, "You used us to pound and grind, but now we shall pound and grind you!"

The dogs said, "You beat us with sticks, you wouldn't give us our food. We couldn't eat because of you. But now we shall eat you!"

The cookpots and griddles said, "You put us in the fire. We are all covered in soot. You burned us, but now we shall burn you!"

Even the hearthstones turned against the wooden people. The hearthstones jumped out of the hearth and threw themselves at the people, and at that the people turned and ran.

The people tried to hide on top of their houses, but the houses fell down. They tried to climb the trees, but the branches broke beneath them. They tried to go into the caves, but the mouths of the caves were shut.

So it was that the people made from wood were destroyed. They turned into monkeys, and went to live in the forests. And thus it is that monkeys look like people, because they come from those creatures made from wood who were but incomplete human beings.

Twice the Creators had tried to make people, and twice they had failed. Once again, they came together and took counsel among themselves, to see what might be done, for soon the sun and moon and stars were going to rise upon the earth. The Creators planned and thought, and finally they said, "Ah! We see what must be done! Now we know what we must use to make people the correct way."

The place that held what was needed to make people was called Broken Place, and also it was called Brackish Water. Inside Broken Place and Brackish Water was maize, both yellow and white. The Creators learned of the maize from four animals. The fox, coyote, parrot, and crow came to the Creators and told them where the yellow and white maize might be found. They showed the Creators how to get into Broken Place. The Creators saw the maize, and thus they know that this was the best thing they could use to make new people. The Creators used the maize to make the bodies, and water to make the blood.

Maize was not the only thing inside Broken Place. Also it held many other good foods. Cacao there was, and the fruits called *zapote* and *anona*, and sour plums. All manner of other fruits there were, and also good sweet honey.

Xmucane, the Grandmother of Light, took the ripe maize. She took both yellow and white kernels and ground them well. She took water and washed her hands with it, and the water that dripped off her hands turned into fat. Xmucane ground the maize nine times, and The One Who Begets and The One Who Bears and the Ruler and the Plumed Serpent together took the maize flour and water, and fashioned it into human beings. And thus it was that the first true people were all made of maize, were all made of food.

The Creators made four people from the maize and water. And these were their names: the first was called Jaguar Quitze; the second was called Jaguar Night; the third was Mahucutah by name; and the fourth was Wind Jaguar. These were the first people, the first ancestors of all who came after, and they had no begetting and no birth. They were made by the Creators, from their thoughts and their labor alone.

15

Once the four first people were made, they were able to talk. They could see what was around them, and hear. They could move about and do their work. They were well made in their bodies, bodies that were those of human males. Their understanding of the world was perfect, and it came to them unbidden and instantly. They could see everything without turning their heads, without going from one place to another. They could even see through the stones and the trees.

The One Who Makes asked the new men, "What do you see, and what do you know? Does your speech please you, and your movement? Tell me what you perceive."

And so, the four first men did look about them, and they saw everything, and they were very pleased. They said to The One Who Makes and The One Who Molds, "We can see and we can hear. We can speak and we can move about. These are the gifts of our Creators, who made us to understand what is far and what is near, what is great and what is small. For this we give thanks to our Grandfather and our Grandmother. We give thanks twice and thrice to the Ones who created us."

When the four first men had thus thanked the Creators, they then understood everything there was to know in the four corners of the world. But The One Who Makes and The One Who Molds said, "It is not good, that our new creatures understand everything so well."

The One Who Bears and The One Who Begets heard the words of the other Creators, and they also looked upon the new people and saw they had too much knowledge. And so, they dimmed the sight of the new people, so that they could only see well those things that were close by. When the four men's sight was dimmed, they also lost their understanding of all things that they had had before.

And thus it was that the first four men were made by the Creators, and were given speech and movement, but who were made to be lesser than the gods.

But the making of the people was not yet perfectly accomplished, for there were no women. So, one night when the four men slept, the

Creators made four women and placed them at the sides of their men. When the men awoke and found their beautiful wives next to them, they rejoiced.

These were the names of the women: Sky Sea House was the wife of Jaguar Quitze; Prawn House was the wife of Jaguar Night; Hummingbird House was the wife of Mahucutah; and Macaw House was the wife of Wind Jaguar. And thus it was that the first four women were made by the Creators, and they became the mothers of all the K'iche' people.

There in the East the people multiplied. There in the East the K'iche' people had their beginnings, with these forefathers and foremothers.

Now the earth and sky had been made, and the earth set apart from the waters. Beasts and birds had been made. The many kinds of good food had been found, and new people were created that could speak and move and work and keep sacred the holy days of the gods. But still the sun and moon and stars had not risen, and all creation was in darkness. All of creation waited for the dawning of the sun.

When the time was ripe, the Morning Star appeared in its brilliance. The people and the birds and the beasts saw it in the sky. It was then that all the creatures knew that the sun would surely rise. And so, the people waited, and they watched, and when they saw the light of the sun begin to shine in the East, they rejoiced greatly. They prepared offerings of copal incense, and they wept as they burnt the incense in thanksgiving for the rising of the sun. At this time, the number of people had become very great, and all the tribes together praised the rising of the sun.

The birds and the beasts also saw the sun. They came out of the canyons and went up to the tops of the mountains to see this new thing, and like the people, the birds and beasts also rejoiced. Seeing the sun rise, the beasts and birds cried out, each one after its own kind. Jaguar roared. Parrot squawked. Birds took to the sky, flying about with great happiness.

The sun was very great and very hot, and he dried up the earth as he rose. At that first rising, all the creatures of the world saw the sun as he truly is; they saw him in all his grandeur and splendor, and in all his unbearable heat. But since that time the sun has diminished himself, so as not to harm the creatures or over-parch the earth.

Upon that mountain, the people made their home, that holy place from which they watched the first sunrise, and from which they first saw the moon and the stars.

And that is the tale of how the world came to be, with the beasts and birds and people that live in it.

## The Creation Tale from *The Books of Chilam Balam*

*Several of the nine* Books of Chilam Balam *that exist today contain related versions of a creation tale. It is in the* Chilam Balam *creation myths that we see some of the diversity of Maya religious belief: the Yucatec story of how the world was made is quite different from that in the K'iche'* Popol Vuh. *For example, although both the Yucatec and K'iche' concepts of divinity include multipartite gods that seem to exist simultaneously as a single, unitary entity, the primary creator gods in these two traditions are different. In the Yucatec myth, creation is carried out by entities known collectively as* Oxlahun-ti-ku *(The Thirteen Gods) and* Bolon-ti-ku *(The Nine Gods), who seem to have been gods of the heavens and the Underworld, respectively, and by deities known as the* Four Bacabs. *The K'iche', by contrast, saw the process of creation as being overseen by a variety of both single and multipartite gods, including Heart of Sky (a trinity) and the Plumed Serpent (a unity).*

*Two technical terms in this story require explanation. First is the phrase "Katun 11 Ahau," which is a calendrical reference. A* katun *is a span of approximately 20 years in the Maya Long Count calendar;* 11 Ahau *designates which katun is meant. The other term is "Peten," a Maya word referring to the land inhabited by the*

*Maya on the Yucatan Peninsula. These two elements locate the story both in place and in time.*

*In reading the Yucatec creation myth presented below, it is important to note that Maya conventions of mythography and storytelling differ from those that most Western readers will be familiar with. These myths were not told and recorded for Western readers: they were made for the Maya, who doubtless considered them very meaningful and sufficient in and of themselves, and whose traditions and culture would have informed their understanding of the story.*

*Some translators and editors of the* Chilam Balam *books present the texts as prose, while others present it in poetic form. I am choosing to present this myth as poetry, since poetry has a flavor and rhythm that seems better suited to the story than prose. Although here I combine several related versions of the Yucatec creation myth into a single story, I did not generally try to smooth over the apparent disjunctures, either of events or of time, that exist in the original.*

In the beginning

There was Oxlahun-ti-ku, The Thirteen Gods.

There was Bolon-ti-ku, The Nine Gods.

There was Itzam Cab Ain, the Great Earth Crocodile.

There was Itzam Cab Ain,

Whose body became the earth,

Whose body became the Peten,

Whose body became the earth upon which the people live

After the great flood,

After the great deluge that destroyed everything,

Before everything was made anew.

It was in Katun 11 Ahau

That Ah Musen Cab went forth.

Ah Musen Cab,

the Lord of the Bees,

Went forth.

He came to Oxlahun-ti-ku,

Ah Musen Cab seized Oxlahun-ti-ku,

He seized The Thirteen Gods

And blindfolded him.

And The Thirteen Gods did not know his name.

This happened after the world had already been made,

But before it was laid waste and created anew.

Oxlahun-ti-ku was blindfold,

And so he was seized by Bolon-ti-ku.

The Lord of the Heavens was blindfold,

Helpless.

And fire came down.

And ropes came down.

And stones and trees came down.

And the Lord of the Netherworld

Came to the one who was blindfolded.

Bolon-ti-ku struck him.

He struck Oxlahun-ti-ku in the head,

He wounded him in the head,

He buffeted him in the face,

He spat on him,

He bound Oxlahun-ti-ku

And laid him on his back,

Helpless.

Bolon-ti-ku took his regalia.

The Lord of the Netherworld

Took the scepter of the Lord of the Heavens,

He took away his ash,

The ash that marks the face of one

Who is fasting,

Who is being purified,

Who is being consecrated.

When Oxlahun-ti-ku was free,

When he was free from his bonds,

He took green shoots,

Shoots of the *yaxum* tree.

He took seeds,

Seeds of squash,

Seeds and beans,

And wrapped them up in the body of Bolon Dz'acab,

In the body of the Lord of Nine Generations.

Oxlahun-ti-ku wrapped up the seeds,

And then ascended to the thirteenth heaven.

When Oxlahun-ti-ku ascended,

On the earth remained only the husks,

On the earth remained only the corn cobs.

The heart of the earth,

The heart of the people was gone

Because of the ascent of Oxlahun-ti-ku,

But the people were in ignorance.

The people were alive on the earth,

But they had no hearts.

The people were alive on the earth,

But they had no fathers,

They had no husbands,

They had no hearts,

And so they were all destroyed,

Together they were all destroyed.

They were buried by sand,

They were drowned in the waves,

The waves of the sea.

When the insignia of The Thirteen Gods was taken,

When he was robbed of his scepter

When he was robbed of his ash,

The ash for penitence

And for consecration,

It was then that the floods came.

It was then that the sky fell.

It was then that the Four Bacabs came forth,

It was then that the Four Bacabs destroyed the world

And remade it anew.

The Four Bacabs planted four mighty trees,

Four mighty trees in the corners of the world,

Four mighty trees in the corners of the Peten.

A red tree for the East,

A white tree for the North,

A black tree for the West,

A yellow tree for the South,

Trees of abundance,

Trees for the nesting of birds,

Trees to hold up the heavens.

And when the Trees of the Four Corners were planted,

The Bacabs went to the center of the world.

They went to the center of the Peten,

And there they planted a great green tree,

The green World-Tree of abundance,

The World-Tree

That records the destruction of the world.

And so it was

After the Trees had been established

That the Morning Star

And the Evening Star

Were set in their places.

The rosy light of dawn in the East

And the fading light of dusk in the West

Were set in their places.

And Lahun Chan who is Ten Sky

Is the Evening Star,

And he is in the West.

And Lahun Chan who is Ten Sky

Is the Morning Star,

And he is in the East.

Then it was that Ah Uuc Cheknal came forth,

That The One Who Fertilizes Maize Seven Times came forth,

He came forth into the seven parts of the world,

He went to Itzam Cab Ain,

And it was then that the heavens touched the earth,

It was then that Itzam Cab Ain was made fertile,

That the earth was made fecund.

At that time there was neither day nor night.

At that time all was in darkness.

At that time there was neither sun nor moon nor stars,

But then the world began to be created.

They saw that the world was being created,

And behold! There was dawn,

And the world was made anew.

# PART II: THE ADVENTURES OF THE HERO TWINS

## The Downfall of Seven Macaw

*The story of the downfall of Seven Macaw is the first of the stories of the Hero Twins, Hunahpu and Xbalanque, in the* Popol Vuh. *In this story, the twins outsmart and defeat a boastful being who dares to think himself greater than the sun. The Hero Twins, as servants of the triune god Heart of Sky, are tasked with putting Seven Macaw in his place. This is important not only because Heart of Sky requires it, but because Hunahpu and Xbalanque are destined to themselves become the sun and the moon, as we see in the story of their battles with the Lords of Death in a later story, and it is not right that Seven Macaw should usurp their position.*

*The names of the twins, Hunahpu and Xbalanque, are difficult to translate into English. In his translation of the* Popol Vuh, *Allen Christenson states that "Hunahpu" can be translated as "One Blowgun Hunter." Christenson notes that "Xbalanque" is rather more difficult to translate. He says that the prefix* x- *can be either a diminutive affix or an indication of feminine gender, while* balan *is probably the same word as* balam, *which means "jaguar," and* q'e *means "sun" in one Kekchi Maya dialect. He also notes that the*

25

*Maya "identified the jaguar with the sun, particularly in its journey through the underworld at night" (p. 81, n. 164). Christenson therefore suggests the translation "Young Hidden/Jaguar Sun" for this name, and notes that it is especially apt given the entry of the Hero Twins into Xibalba, the Maya Underworld, in a later story in the* Popol Vuh.

In the time of the people made of wood, in the time when they were destroyed in the great flood, and in the time before the rising of the sun and moon and stars, there was a being called Seven Macaw. And although there was no light from the sun or moon or stars, there was a light from Seven Macaw, for he was a great being.

But Seven Macaw was over-proud of his greatness. He boasted long and loud about how great he was. He said, "What need have the people of sun and moon? I can make all the light they need, for I am truly great. I have eyes all made of bright jewels. I have teeth all made of bright jewels. My nest is made of shining metal. My feathers are made of shining metal. My greatness shines all over the whole earth." And so, he puffed himself up and boasted of his greatness, even though he could not see the whole world but only to the horizon.

At that time also there were two boys, twins named Hunahpu and Xbalanque, and they were both gods. They saw how Seven Macaw puffed himself up. They heard how he boasted of his greatness. The twins said to one another, "It is not good that Seven Macaw goes about boasting like this. It is not good that he praises himself so loudly before Heart of Sky. People will not be able to be created, or be able to live on the earth, with Seven Macaw doing as he does. People cannot live properly where jewels and precious metals are the most important things. Let us take our blowguns and put an end to Seven Macaw and all his boasting and all his riches."

And so, the twins took up their blowguns and set out to find Seven Macaw to put an end to him.

Now, Seven Macaw had two sons of his own, and these were Zipacna and Cabracan. And Seven Macaw had also a wife, whose name was Chimalmat, and she was the mother of his sons. Zipacna made great mountains, and Cabracan, whose name means "earthquake," shook them. Zipacna and Cabracan had the same fault of pride as their father did.

Seven Macaw said, "I am great! I am the sun!"

Zipacna said, "I am great! I make the mountains!"

Cabracan said, "I am great! I make the sky tremble and shake the mountains down!"

Hunahpu and Xbalanque saw how Zipacna and Cabracan boasted, just like their father did. The twins saw that this was evil, and they swore that they also would put an end to Seven Macaw's sons.

The favorite food of Seven Macaw was the nance fruit. Every day, he would go to the nance tree and sit in the boughs to eat the fruit. Hunahpu and Xbalanque found out where Seven Macaw liked to eat his meal. They arrived before him, and lay in wait for him. When Seven Macaw ascended the tree and began to eat, Hunahpu took up his blowgun and aimed a shot at Seven Macaw. The dart went right into Seven Macaw's jaw, and the force of it knocked him out of the tree. Hunahpu came running up to Seven Macaw, thinking to grab him. But instead Seven Macaw grabbed Hunahpu by the arm and bent it back, back, back. Seven Macaw pulled and pulled. He pulled Hunahpu's arm right out of its socket, and then ran away home, carrying Hunahpu's arm with him.

When Seven Macaw arrived home, his wife Chimalmat said, "Whatever happened to you? What is wrong with your jaw? And what is that you carry?"

Seven Macaw replied, "I was in the nance tree having my meal when two demons shot me. They shot me in the jaw, and now it is all broken, my teeth are all broken, and it hurts. But I showed them. I tore the arm of one of them out of its socket. I shall hang it over the fireplace until they decide to come and get it back." Then he took Hunahpu's arm and hung it over the fireplace, as he said he would do.

After Seven Macaw left with Hunahpu's arm, the twins took thought as to what they should do next. They decided they needed to get Hunahpu's arm back. They also knew they would need help to do this. Hunahpu and Xbalanque went looking for a very old grandfather who had white hair and a very humble grandmother. The grandfather's name was Great White Peccary. The grandmother's name was Great White Tapir. They were both very, very old.

Hunahpu and Xbalanque asked the grandmother and grandfather for help. The twins said, "We are going to get Hunahpu's arm back from Seven Macaw. You will tell Seven Macaw that we are your grandchildren, and that your work is curing people of toothache. That way we will trick Seven Macaw into thinking that we are mere children."

The grandparents agreed to help the twins and to do as they said.

And so Hunahpu and Xbalanque set out for Seven Macaw's house with the grandmother and grandfather. The old ones went in front. The twins went behind, playing and running about as though they were mere children. They came to Seven Macaw's house, where Seven Macaw was crying aloud with pain from his teeth and jaw. Seven Macaw saw the grandparents and the twins and said, "Where are you going? Are those your children?"

The grandfather said, "We travel about and ply our trade, my lord. And these are our grandchildren. Sadly, their parents are dead, and we must care for them."

Fighting through the pain in his mouth, Seven Macaw said, "Have pity on me, help me! Perhaps you know some way to cure the pain in my jaw, to cure what is wrong with my eyes. Can you help me?"

"We pull rotten teeth, my lord," said the grandparents, "and we cure eye diseases and set bones. Yes, we can help you."

"Oh, please, please cure my mouth," said Seven Macaw. "Heal my jaw. Fix my loose teeth. They hurt so badly I cannot eat. I cannot sleep. Also cure my eyes. I was shot by two demons, and how I have suffered ever since!"

"Ah," said the grandparents, "we shall have to remove the loose teeth in order to cure them. That is the way to cure the ills in your mouth."

Seven Macaw said, "I do not want you to pull my teeth. They are all made of precious jewels. And I will not look so fine without teeth in my mouth."

"Have no fear, my lord," said the grandparents. "We shall give you replacement teeth, even though they will be made of ground bone."

"Do what you must," said Seven Macaw, "but be sure you give me new replacement teeth."

The grandparents pulled out all of Seven Macaw's teeth, each one of them a precious jewel. And then they placed the replacement teeth in his mouth. But here they tricked him, for the teeth were not made of bone, as they had said, but of grains of white maize. Then the grandparents cured Seven Macaw's eyes. They took from his eyes all the jewels and precious metals that had been there. They took away all the things that had made him beautiful and proud. And then Seven Macaw's pain was gone, but he no longer looked fine and lordly, and he died from the shame of it, and his wife Chimalmat died with him.

Then the grandparents took Hunahpu's arm from the place Seven Macaw had hung it, and they reattached it. Soon enough, Hunahpu was good as new.

And so it was that Hunahpu and Xbalanque did the will of Heart of Sky. They brought about the downfall of Seven Macaw, whose pride had made him evil.

## The Downfall of Zipacna

*In his translation of the* Popol Vuh, *Allen Christensen notes the ritual and cultural significance of the house lintel in Maya culture. According to Christensen, Maya people consider house lintels to have great power, and that Zipacna's transgression was taking up a powerful ritual object by himself without permission and without having first been ritually prepared to do so. It is this that leads the four hundred boys to sentence him to death, and gives the Hero Twins a legitimate reason to kill him.*

*Christensen also notes that Zipacna's name might have derived from* cipactli, *the Nahuatl word for "crocodile." If so, Christenson states, then Zipacna is himself a crocodile. Since crocodiles are not particularly mobile when they are on their backs, part of the Hero Twins' trick against Zipacna involves getting him onto his back, a position where he is vulnerable despite his great strength.*

Zipacna was the son of Seven Macaw. Zipacna was a maker of mountains, and a very strong giant. One day, Zipacna was bathing in the river when a group of four hundred boys passed by, dragging with them the trunk of a great tree. This was hard work for the boys, for the trunk was very big and very heavy.

Zipacna called out to them. He said, "What are you doing? Why do you carry that tree?"

The boys replied, "We have cut down this tree to make a lintel to put atop the doorway for our house. But it is so heavy, we cannot lift it. We cannot carry it."

Zipacna said, "Let me help you," and he took the great trunk of the tree up onto his shoulders and carried it to the place where the boys were building their house. Zipacna then helped them put the lintel onto their house.

When that was done, the boys said, "Do you have a mother or father?"

"I have neither," said Zipacna, for both Seven Macaw, his father, and Chimalmat, his mother, were dead.

"Then stay with us," said the boys, "and you can help us get another tree to use for building our house."

And so Zipacna agreed to stay with the boys and to help them get another tree. But behind Zipacna's back, the boys plotted against him. "Who does he think he is, lifting our log like that all by himself? We should kill him."

The boys decided to dig a great hole and ask Zipacna to get inside it. Then they would drop the tree on his head and kill him with it. When the hole was dug, they went to Zipacna and said, "We need this hole to go deeper, but we can't do that work ourselves. Will you do it for us?"

Zipacna agreed to dig. "Call us when you have dug down far enough," said the boys, and they left him to his work, thinking that they would throw the log in when Zipacna called. But Zipacna had heard the plans of the boys. He knew they intended to kill him. So instead of digging down, he dug into the side of the hole. He dug a small chamber in which to hide, in which to save himself when the boys tried to kill him.

The boys came to the hole and called down, "Are you finished digging yet?"

Zipacna replied, "Not quite yet. I shall call you when the hole is deep enough."

Zipacna kept digging until he had made a chamber big enough to hide in. Then he went into the chamber and called out to the boys. "The hole is deep enough! Please help me take away all the earth I dug. You should see how far down I have dug!"

The boys heard Zipacna's call. They took up the great tree and dragged it to the lip of the hole. They tipped the tree into the hole. Down it went, hitting the bottom with a mighty *thump*. And when the tree hit the bottom of the hole, Zipacna cried out as though in agony.

"Ha! He is dead!" said the boys, and they danced about with happiness at their victory. "It is good that we killed him," they said to one another, "because he was too strong, and he might have tried to rule us without our consent."

Then the boys decided that they would make some good liquor to drink, that they would do that for three days, and that during the three days, they would check to make sure that the giant was indeed dead. They would know he was dead when the ants began to gather in the hole. When the drink was made, and the ants had gathered, and they were sure Zipacna was dead, they would then hold a great celebration.

Zipacna sat in the chamber he had dug, and from that hole in the earth, he heard all the plans of the boys. He knew he had to convince them that he was dead. He cut his nails. He trimmed his hair. The ants came down the hole and found the hair and nail clippings. They took these up, and began taking them back to their nest.

After three days, the boys went to the hole and saw the ants carrying pieces of Zipacna's nails and hair. They said, "Surely the giant is dead! See? The ants are carrying his nails and hair. Now we may have our celebration."

The boys went into their house and drank their sweet liquor until they were drunk. When Zipacna was sure they were so drunk they would not hear him coming, he climbed out of the hole and pulled the house down upon their heads, killing them all. Not one of the four hundred boys survived. They were taken up into the heavens and became the constellation called Motz (Pleiades).

Now, it soon came to the ears of Hunahpu and Xbalanque that Zipacna had killed the four hundred boys. This made the twins very angry, for the boys had been their friends. They vowed to take revenge on Zipacna for his deed. The twins knew that during the day, Zipacna would be at the river catching fish and crabs, while at night he went about carrying mountains from place to place. The twins vowed they would trick him by using his love for crab meat. They took up some leaves and flowers of the bromeliad plant and used these to make the legs and claws, while a great stone became the body. The twins hid the false crab in a cave that was under a mountain called Meauan. Then they went looking for Zipacna.

The twins went along the river, guessing that this was the most likely place the giant would be during the day, and soon enough they found him there, fishing for crab as was his wont. "What are you doing there?" they asked him.

Zipacna replied, "I am fishing for crabs to eat."

"Have you caught any?" said the twins.

"No," said Zipacna. "I haven't had any luck for days, and I am ravenously hungry."

"Oh!" said the twins. "Oh, we know where there is a great crab that you could eat. We saw it just a little while ago, in a cave not far from here. We tried to catch it, but its claws were too strong and we had to let it go. But you seem like a very strong fellow; perhaps you could catch the crab."

"Yes!" said Zipacna. "I could catch a great crab like that with ease! Please, show me how to get to the cave."

"We have other business to tend to and cannot show you," said the twins, "but if you follow the river westward to the base of that mountain over there, you'll find the cave very easily. The crab is quite large, so you should have no difficulty finding it."

"Oh, please, please, show me the way!" cried Zipacna. "What if I get lost and cannot find the cave? I have not eaten in so long, I am very weak. Besides, if you come with me, maybe you will find birds to shoot with your blowguns along the way, and then we shall all have something good to eat today."

When the boys saw how desperate Zipacna was, they agreed to take him to the cave. Together the three walked westward along the river until they came to the place where the twins had hidden the false crab. Zipacna saw the claws showing near the mouth of the cave. He lay down on his stomach to climb in, for the mouth of the cave was very narrow. He crawled forward head first, but the false crab moved away, and he could not catch it. Zipacna came out of the cave empty-handed.

"Did you not catch the crab?" the twins asked.

"No, it moved away when I got close," said Zipacna.

"Perhaps if you go in on your back you will have better luck," said the twins.

"Yes, that is a good idea," said Zipacna. "I will try doing that."

Zipacna lay on his back and squirmed his way into the mouth of the cave. He wriggled in up to his shoulders, then up to his waist. But when he had gone in up to his knees, the mountain settled down on top of him, and he could not get out. And in this way, Hunahpu and Xbalanque put an end to Zipacna, son of Seven Macaw, there in the west of the world.


**The Downfall of Cabracan**

*Guatemala is part of the Pacific Ring of Fire, and its western mountain range and southwestern plain are dotted with volcanoes. Guatemala therefore experiences frequent earthquakes, so it is no surprise that the Maya would have created a myth surrounding those frightening and potentially destructive natural events.*

*The story of the downfall of Cabracan, whose name is the Maya word for "earthquake," is a combination of a cautionary tale against excessive pride and a trickster tale. It also may be a kind of just-so story, since according to Allen Christensen, the Maya even today conceptualize earthquakes as the thrashings of a giant who is buried underground.*

Cabracan was the second son of the prideful Seven Macaw. "I am the strongest!" proclaimed Cabracan. "I shake the very mountains! I bring them tumbling down!"

Heart of Sky looked down from the heavens and saw Cabracan knocking down mountains and boasting about it. "This is not right," said Heart of Sky. "This boasting is very bad indeed. He is making out that he is even greater than the sun. I shall have to do something about this."

And so, Heart of Sky went to the Hero Twins, Hunahpu and Xbalanque. He told the twins that Cabracan had become so prideful that he must be killed. "Cabracan thinks he is more important even than the sun," Heart of Sky said to the twins, "and so you must put an end to him. Bring him to the east, where the sun rises, and deal with him there."

"We will do this thing, O Heart of Sky," said the twins, "for we also disapprove of his boastful behavior, and it is our duty to do your will."

Hunahpu and Xbalanque went looking for Cabracan. They soon found him, shaking mountains down as was his wont. Cabracan was so powerful that all he needed to do was tap his foot and down would come the mountain; nothing would be left but rubble and dust.

The twins said to Cabracan, "Where are you going?"

Cabracan said, "I'm not going anywhere. I'm knocking mountains down, turning them into rubble and dust. That is what I like to do."

Then Cabracan looked closely at the twins. "I don't think I've seen you before. Where are you from? What are your names?"

"We have no names," said the twins. "We are simply poor hunters. We wander through the mountains with our blowguns looking for game. But if you're looking for mountains to flatten, maybe you should go over there. We saw a great mountain there, so large that it towers over all the others. We tried and tried to catch birds on that mountain, but we had no luck. Do you really knock mountains down?"

"Yes, I certainly do," said Cabracan. "But tell me more of this mountain. I don't see how I could have missed one that big."

"It is in the east," said the twins.

"Take me there," said Cabracan.

And so, they set out on their road together, with Cabracan in the middle and one twin on either side of him. As they walked, the twins hunted birds with their blowguns. The guns had no pellets in them. All the twins had to do was point the gun at a bird and blow, and down the bird would fall, dead. Cabracan watched the twins, and marveled at how they could kill the birds with just the force of their breath.

When the boys had killed enough birds, they stopped to cook and eat them. The boys made a fire, and began to roast some of the birds on a spit. One bird they set aside. This they covered in earth, to use to trick Cabracan. They said, "When he becomes hungry, we will give him this one to eat. When he eats the bird covered in earth, it will make him weak, and we will be able to defeat him. Cabracan will be buried in the earth, just as the bird he eats will become buried inside him."

After a time, the rich aroma of roasting bird filled the air. The skins of the birds became golden brown. Rich fat dripped into the fire and sizzled, casting up fragrant smoke. Cabracan smelled the goodness of the roasting birds. He became very hungry, and his mouth watered greatly. "What is this you are cooking?" he said. "It smells so good; let me have some."

"Certainly," said the twins, and they handed to him the bird they had smeared with earth.

The giant was so hungry that he swallowed the bird in one bite. He did not even notice that it had been covered with earth. He ate the bird, earth, skin, meat, bones, and all.

When the three had finished their meal, they continued their journey eastward. Cabracan felt strange. His limbs felt tired and weak. He could not understand what was happening. The enchanted bird covered in earth was doing its work. Soon they came to the mountain.

"There it is!" said the twins. "Bring down the mountain!"

Cabracan tried to shake the mountain, but he could not do anything to it. He was so weak that he sank down to the ground. The twins grabbed Cabracan and bound his hands behind his back. They also bound his ankles together. Then the twins dug a great pit. They cast Cabracan into it, and filled the pit with earth, and there the giant died. And so Cabracan, the son of Seven Macaw, was brought down by the Hero Twins, Hunahpu and Xbalanque, there in the east of the world.

# The History of the Hero Twins

*In addition to the three stories of the Hero Twins' victories over Seven Macaw and his sons, the* Popol Vuh *contains an extended tale of the twins' parentage and their exploits in Xibalba, the Maya Underworld. That the twins are divine beings is attested by not only their superhuman powers but also by their blood relationship to several Maya deities, and by the unusual nature of their conception.*

*Hunahpu's and Xbalanque's father is One Hunahpu, the son of Xmucane, the Grandmother of Light and one of the deities involved in the creation of the world, as we saw above. Their mother is Lady Blood, who is the daughter of Gathered Blood, one of the Lords of the Underworld. The twins are conceived when the head of One Hunahpu, who has been killed, drools saliva into Lady Blood's hand. The Maya story therefore shares with many other traditions, including those of the Aztecs and the ancient Irish, the idea that divine beings can be conceived without coitus.*

*The sacred ballgame, which the Maya called* pitz *and the Aztecs knew as* tlatchtli, *plays a central role in the greater part of the Hunahpu and Xbalanque stories, and was an important feature of Mesoamerican social and ritual life. This game, which involved play on an I-shaped court with raised walls, used a solid rubber ball which the players had to hit with their hips, knees, or elbows through a stone hoop that was affixed to the walls of the long sides of the court.*

*The twins embody some of the most common traits of divine heroes. They are prodigiously strong, skilled, clever, and can work a certain amount of magic. They can speak to animals and understand what the animals say to them. They also are superb tricksters: they not only manage to get out of tight spots that were the downfall of their own elders, but also to defeat the Lords of Death by means of a trick.*

### One Hunahpu and Seven Hunahpu in Xibalba

You have heard of the great deeds of Hunahpu and Xbalanque, and how they defeated the boastful Seven Macaw and his sons, Zipacna and Cabracan. And now you shall hear of the deeds of their father, and of how Hunahpu and Xbalanque were born, and of the deeds of the twins and their father in Xibalba, which is the Underworld, the Land of Death.

Two brothers there were, One Hunahpu and Seven Hunahpu, and they were the sons of Xmucane, the Grandmother of Light, who assisted with the creation of humankind. One Hunahpu was the father of Hunahpu and Xbalanque, but he also had two other sons, named One Batz and One Chouen, which mean One Monkey and One Artisan, and these were born long before the Hero Twins. One Hunahpu's wife was named Xbaquiyalo, which means Egret Woman, but she died very soon.

Seven Hunahpu had no wife, but lived with his brother as a companion and servant. Both One Hunahpu and Seven Hunahpu were wise and knowledgeable. They were men of good hearts, seers who could tell the future. They taught all they knew to One Monkey and One Artisan, and thus the boys played well upon the flute and sang with sweet voices. They knew how to make beautiful things from jade and silver and gold. They wrote well, and could sculpt in stone.

One Hunahpu and Seven Hunahpu liked to spend their days playing at dice and the sacred ball game. Every day they would go down to the ballcourt to practice. Sometimes One Monkey and One Artisan would join their father and uncle, and together the four of them would play game after game against one another. They were all very skilled ballplayers. At the times when they all played the game together, Voc, the Falcon, who is the messenger of Heart of Sky, would come to watch them.

Now, the ballcourt of One Hunahpu and Seven Hunahpu was directly over the road to Xibalba. Whenever the men and the twins played ball, the thudding of their feet and the thumping of the ball against ground and wall and bodies would echo through the halls of the Underworld. One day, the brothers and the twins played a very hard game of ball. The thudding and thumping were even louder than usual as they tried to defeat one another. It was so loud and so distracting that the Lords of Xibalba, One Death and Seven Death, said to one another, "What is all the racket they make up there? This is so disrespectful. They should not make such noise. We'll show them what it means to respect the Lords of Xibalba. We will invite them to play that noisy game down here. We will show them who the best ballplayers in the whole world are, and when we do, they won't be able to play anymore, and our realm will be peaceful and quiet once again."

First One Death and Seven Death called to themselves all the judges and demons of Xibalba, and these are their names and duties:

Flying Scab and Gathered Blood make people ill in their blood.

Pus Demon and Jaundice Demon make the skin turn yellow and cause the body to swell and ooze pus.

Bone Staff and Skull Staff bear staffs made of bone. Their duty is to cause people to waste away until they are nothing but skin and bones.

Trash Demon and Stab Demon attacked people who did not clean the trash from around their houses, those who did not sweep their thresholds and keep the space around their homes clean and tidy. These demons would descend upon those people and stab them until they died.

The last two judges of Xibalba were called Wing and Packstrap. They afflicted those who traveled the roads, and those who walked the roads carrying heavy burdens. Wing and Packstrap made these people die vomiting blood.

And so, the Lords of Xibalba told the judges and demons what they were going to do. They said, "One Hunahpu and Seven Hunahpu do not respect us. They play their ballgame very noisily. We are going to challenge them to a ballgame to make them stop. What say you?"

The judges and demons replied, "This is a good thought. These are good words. We also are weary of the noise they make. Also, we desire to have their ballgame equipment, their pads and masks, and their ball. Yes, let us play the ballgame with them and show them who the true champions are. We can win from them their gaming things. Then they will not be able to play, and perhaps we shall have some peace and quiet."

When the judges and demons had agreed to the plan, the Lords of Xibalba next called to themselves their messenger Owls. They sent the Owls to One Hunahpu and Seven Hunahpu, commanding them to come to Xibalba to play the ballgame there and to bring with them all their gaming equipment. One Hunahpu and Seven Hunahpu accepted the summons, but before they left, they told One Monkey and One Artisan to stay with their Grandmother, Xmucane, to look after her. They also told the boys to continue practicing their arts.

Xmucane was very frightened when she heard what One Hunahpu and Seven Hunahpu had been called upon to do. She wept most bitterly. "O my sons," she said, "surely I will never see you again. Surely the Lords of Xibalba will never let you go. Please don't leave me here alone."

"Never fear, Mother," said the brothers. "We will return. This we promise you. And while we are gone, One Monkey and One Artisan will care for you as well as we have always done."

And so, One Hunahpu and Seven Hunahpu took up their gaming things to go to play the Lords of Death. But they left behind their rubber ball, which they tied to the top of their house. Then taking their leave of their mother and the twins, they followed the Owls to the entrance of Xibalba.

It was a long and weary road to Xibalba. The Owls led the brothers down a long flight of stairs that went to the bottom of a canyon. Two canyons they had to pass through. The brothers also had to cross many dangerous rivers. One river was full of scorpions. Another was made all of blood, and another made all of pus. But the brothers crossed them all without coming to harm.

After crossing all the rivers, the brothers came to a place where four roads met. There was a white road that led north, a yellow road that led south, a red road that led east, and a black road that led west. The brothers did not know which road to take, until they heard a strange whisper coming up from the ground. "I am the black road," said the whispering voice. "It is my path you must tread to the place you are going."

At last the brothers arrived at the council chamber of the Lords of Xibalba. There they saw two seated figures. "Greetings, O One Death," they said. "Greetings, O Seven Death."

But the figures made no reply. One Hunahpu and Seven Hunahpu were very puzzled, until they heard rasping, gargling laughter coming from inside the chamber. Then they realized that the figures in front of the chamber were nothing but wooden statues meant to fool them.

"Come in, come in!" said the Lords of Death. "Do not mind our little joke. Come in!"

The brothers went into the chamber where the Lords of Death awaited them along with all the judges and demons.

"Sit down!" said the Lords of Death, showing the brothers a bench. "You must be weary after your long journey. We will play the ballgame tomorrow. Please, sit down!"

One Hunahpu and Seven Hunahpu went to the bench and sat down, but they immediately jumped up again. The bench was made of stone, and it was red hot. The brothers could not sit on it; the stone burned their buttocks. Again, all the Xibalbans roared with laughter. They laughed and laughed until tears ran down their cheeks and their ribs hurt.

When the Lords of Death and the other Xibalbans were finally done with their merriment, they told the brothers that they would be taken to a place where they could spend the night. Now, the Land of the Dead has many Houses within it, and in each House is a different kind of trial.

The House of Darkness contains nothing but the black of night, a night without moon and without stars. It is completely dark within.

The House of Ice is a house of cold. The inside is rimed with frost, and a freezing wind continually blows through it.

The House of Jaguars is full of jaguars. The jaguars prowl about. They have sharp teeth and claws with which to rend and tear.

The House of Bats is full of bats that flitter and flutter all about. They never rest, but fly about squeaking.

The House of Knives is full of sharpened blades that slide back and forth.

The Lords of Death decided that the brothers should be placed in the House of Darkness. "Here is a torch, and here are cigars for you," said the Lords of Death. "Mind that you do not use them all up, for they do not belong to you. Mind that you give them back to us in the morning, just as you receive them now."

And so, One Hunahpu and Seven Hunahpu passed the night in the House of Darkness, watching as the torch and cigars slowly burned away until nothing was left.

In the morning, the Lords of Death came to fetch the brothers for the ballgame. They opened the door to the House of Darkness and said, "Good morning! It is time for our game, but first you must give back the torch and the cigars."

"We cannot, Lords," said the brothers, "for they have all burnt quite away during the night."

"What?" said One Death and Seven Death. "We told you to return them. You have not followed our instructions. You have destroyed our belongings. Therefore, you must die!"

The Lords of Xibalba took the brothers away and sacrificed them. They cut off the head of One Hunahpu, and then buried the rest of his body together with his brother. One Death and Seven Death commanded that One Hunahpu's head be placed in the branches of a tree that stood near the road. As soon as the head was placed there, the tree suddenly began to bear fruit, even though it had never done so before, and the head of One Hunahpu changed to look so much like the fruit that no one could tell where the head was any longer. This is how the calabash tree began to bear fruit, and it is why its fruit is like a human head.

The Xibalbans gathered around the tree, amazed that it had begun to bear fruit so suddenly, simply because One Hunahpu's head had been placed there. And so, the Xibalbans made a law that no one was to take the fruit of that tree, and no one was to take shelter in its shade, on account of the power of One Hunahpu's head.

*Lady Blood and the Tree of One Hunahpu*

Once there was a maiden named Lady Blood, and she was the daughter of a lord named Gathered Blood. One day, her father came home with a strange tale to tell: it was the story of the calabash tree in Xibalba, and how it had begun to bear fruit on account of One Hunahpu's head having been placed in it. After Lady Blood had heard the story, she could think of nothing else but the calabash tree. She longed to see it and to taste of its fruit, and no matter how hard her father tried, no matter how much he warned her about the law against touching the tree or standing in its shade, he could not change his daughter's mind, nor distract her from her desire for the fruit of the calabash tree.

Finally, Lady Blood's desire became so strong she could stand it no longer. She went down the road to the place where the calabash tree was. She stood before the tree and looked longingly upon its fruit. "That fruit seems very good indeed," she said. "I should pick one and eat it. No harm will come to me, I am sure."

A voice replied from the midst of the branches, the voice of the skull of One Hunahpu. "Why should you desire a skull that has been placed in the branches of a tree? That is not something desirable."

"Maybe not, but I wish to have one all the same," said the maiden.

"Very well," said the skull. "Put out your right hand. Put it among the branches of the tree where I can see it."

Lady Blood did as the skull instructed, but instead of receiving a calabash fruit, she felt something wet dripping into her palm: the skull had dribbled some saliva onto her hand. The maiden pulled back her hand to see what had dripped there, but when she looked, she saw nothing at all.

"Have no fear," said the skull, "it is only my spittle that I have given to you, and in the spittle of kings are the descendants of kings. When a man is alive, he has beauty because his bones are covered in flesh, but the bones of the dead are frightening. The essence of the man, especially if he be a great lord, is in his spittle, and thus is his essence passed on to his children. The essence of the lord, and his face, and his speech, continue in the bodies of his sons and daughters. And so shall it be for me, for I have given you my spittle.

It is time now for you to return to your home. You will come to no harm, and you will see that I have spoken the truth to you."

And thus was the will of Heart of Sky accomplished in the meeting of Lady Blood and the skull of One Hunahpu.

After giving Lady Blood other instructions, One Hunahpu bade her return home. She did so, and not long afterward, she found that she was with child. This had been accomplished when the skull spit into her hand, and this was how the Hero Twins Hunahpu and Xbalanque were conceived.

Lady Blood was able to hide her condition for six months, but after that time she began to show. Gathered Blood noticed his daughter was with child, and he became angry. He went before One Death and Seven Death and the other lords of Xibalba and told them that his daughter had lain with a man and now was with child.

"Go and ask her what happened," said the lords of Xibalba. "Get the truth from her. And if she is not truthful, she will be sacrificed."

Gathered Blood agreed that this was a good plan. He returned home and asked his daughter how it was that she was with child. He asked her who the father was, which man she had lain with.

"I have never lain with a man, Father," said Lady Blood. "I don't know what you are talking about."

"So it is true, then," said Gathered Blood. "You are nothing but a common whore."

Gathered Blood summoned the four Owls of Xibalba. When they arrived, Gathered Blood said, "Take that common whore away and sacrifice her. Bring back her heart in a bowl."

The Owls grasped the young woman in their talons. Taking also with them a bowl and a flint knife, they carried Lady Blood through the skies of Xibalba to the place of sacrifice.

"You cannot kill me," said Lady Blood. "I am with child, but not because I have lain with a man. This is the child that was given to me by the skull of One Hunahpu, which rests in the calabash tree, the one that stands next to the road near the ballcourt. I do not deserve to be sacrificed."

"We do not want to sacrifice you," said the Owls, "but we must bring something back in the bowl. What should we do?"

"Go to the croton tree," said Lady Blood. "Gather its sap, for it looks like blood. Gather its sap, and it will look like a heart when it is placed in the bowl."

The Owls did what the young woman told them. They went to the tree. Lady Blood stabbed it with the Owls' sacred flint knife. Red sap oozed out. The Owls caught the sap in the bowl, and there it formed a lump. The sap came together, and it became a rounded shape that looked like a heart.

"Wait here," said the Owls. "Wait here for us. We will go show this to the Lords of Xibalba, and when they are satisfied that you have been sacrificed, we will return to guide you away from here. We will guide you to a place of safety."

And so, the Owls flew back to the Lords of Xibalba with the bowl full of sap. When they arrived, One Death said, "Is that the heart of the young woman in that bowl?"

"It is," said the Owls. "It most truly is."

"Bring it here that I may examine it," said One Death.

The Owls brought the bowl to One Death. He put his fingers into the red sap. He stirred the sap with his fingers, then held them up and looked at them. His fingers seemed to drip with blood.

"Build up the fire," said One Death. "Build it up to burn more hotly. Then we shall burn the heart upon it."

The Owls poked the fire and added wood to it. When it was blazing well, One Death put the sap into it. The sap smoked up with a sweet fragrance. All the Xibalbans gathered around the fire to smell the fragrance of the burning sap, which they all thought was blood. And this is how Lady Blood tricked the Lords of Xibalba.

Now, while the Lords of Xibalba were smelling the fragrance of the tree sap, the Owls returned to Lady Blood and guided her to the world above. Then the Owls went back to Xibalba.

Lady Blood went to the home of Xmucane, the Grandmother of Light, who was the mother of One Hunahpu and Seven Hunahpu and the grandmother of One Monkey and One Artisan. Lady Blood went before Xmucane and said, "I greet you, O Mother, for I am your daughter-in-law."

Xmucane was astonished. "How can this be? My sons descended into Xibalba and never returned, and I am sure that they must be dead. I have only my grandsons, One Monkey and One Artisan. They are all that I have left of my own beloved sons. What you say cannot be true. Go away. Go back to where you came from."

"I speak truth," said Lady Blood. "I am with child, I carry twins, and they are the sons of One Hunahpu. One Hunahpu and Seven Hunahpu are not dead. You will see them again. You will see them when my two children are born."

"No, you lie," said Xmucane. "You lie. My sons are dead. Those cannot be their children. You lay with some man, and now you come to me thinking I will believe you. I do not. Go away."

"I speak truth," said Lady Blood. "Truly these are the sons of One Hunahpu."

"If you really are my daughter-in-law," said Xmucane, "you must prove it. Take this net, and fill it with maize. Do that task successfully, and I will accept that you are my daughter-in-law."

"I will do as you ask," said Lady Blood.

Lady Blood took the net. She went to the field where the maize grew, the field that belonged to One Monkey and One Artisan. Lady Blood went into the field and started looking for maize to fill her net.

She looked and looked, and although the maize was growing well, she could only find one ear to take home. No matter how she searched, she could find no more than one ear of maize that was ready to eat. "Oh, no!" cried Lady Blood. "What shall I do? Surely I have done wrong, for I cannot bring back a netful of maize to my mother-in-law. There is no maize. What shall I do?"

Then Lady Blood began to sing. She sang a song calling on the goddesses of the maize field. "Come, O Lady Thunder!" she sang. "Come, O Yellow Lady! Come, Lady of Cacao! Come, Lady of Cornmeal! Come to my aid, O guardians of the field of One Monkey and One Artisan."

Lady Blood took the corn silk at the top of the ear between her fingers. She pulled gently at the corn silk, without opening the husk, without taking the ear off the stalk. Gently and gently she pulled, and as she pulled, ripe ears of maize tumbled down from the silk into her net. The maize multiplied and multiplied, and still the single ear of maize was untouched upon the stalk. Finally, the young woman had enough maize to fill her net, but how to carry it? It was very full and very heavy, and Grandmother Xmucane's house was a long walk away. But soon the problem was solved: animals came from out of the trees to help her. They took up the net and the pack frame, and they carried it back along the path. But when they came within sight of Xmucane, they handed it back to Lady Blood, who took it up and pretended she had carried it the whole way herself.

When Xmucane saw Lady Blood carrying the heavy net full of maize, she was astonished. "Where did you find all that maize? Did you steal it from some other field? I am going to the field of One Monkey and One Artisan. I will see whether you truly got the maize from there or from some other field."

Xmucane went down the path to the maize field, and there she saw the plant with only one ear upon it, and the other plants with no ripened ears at all. She looked down at the ground underneath the plant with one ear. There she saw the grooves of the strings of the net that were pushed into the soil as the maize came tumbling down from the corn silk, the depression in the soil from the heaviness of the great pile of maize. Then Xmucane understood what had happened, and she returned home.

Xmucane went to Lady Blood and said, "I see now that you have spoken truly. You are my daughter-in-law, and those are my grandsons that you carry."

### The Boyhood Deeds of Hunahpu and Xbalanque

When the time came for the twins to be born, Lady Blood went into the mountains. It was there the twins were born. They came suddenly; their grandmother did not have time to arrive to see them born. Lady Blood named the boys Hunahpu and Xbalanque, and she took them down the mountain to live in Grandmother Xmucane's house with their older brothers One Monkey and One Artisan. But this was not easy for anyone, for the twins wailed constantly, and no one was able to get any sleep.

Finally, Xmucane had had enough. "Take those two babies away! Take them someplace else! No one in this house gets any sleep with them here."

Lady Blood took the boys to an anthill. The ants scurried to and fro, in and out of their anthill. Lady Blood put the twins on the anthill, and they instantly stopped crying and went to sleep.

Another time when the twins were wailing, One Monkey and One Artisan took them and put them in a thorn bush. Again, the baby twins went right to sleep. "We should leave them there," said One Monkey and One Artisan. "We should leave them in the thorns, or on the anthill. Maybe they will die there, and we will have some peace." They said this because they were seers and knew all that would happen to Hunahpu and Xbalanque, and all they would accomplish. One Monkey and One Artisan wished their brothers would die because they were sorely jealous, despite all their own great skills and gifts.

And so it was that Hunahpu and Xbalanque grew up outdoors in the mountains, and not in their grandmother's house. The twins grew well and strong, and soon they were able to go hunting. Every day they went into the forest to hunt birds for their family to eat, and they always came back with something good. One Monkey and One Artisan, however, sat around the house and played their flutes. They did not help with the hunting. They practiced their writing and carving, and they sang. They were very wise, for they had become the face of their father, One Hunahpu, who had been defeated by the Lords of Death in Xibalba. But nothing ever came of their great skills, because their hearts were eaten up with envy, their hearts burned hot with jealousy of Hunahpu and Xbalanque.

When Xmucane would prepare food, One Monkey and One Artisan would eat first. Hunahpu and Xbalanque waited in the doorway for the leftovers. When Hunahpu and Xbalanque brought birds from the forest, One Monkey and One Artisan would snatch them away and eat them, and give nothing to their younger brothers. The twins received no love from their older brothers, nor did they receive any from their grandmother. But Hunahpu and Xbalanque did not become angry. They understood how things were in their grandmother's house. Instead they bided their time, waiting for an opportunity for justice.

One day, Hunahpu and Xbalanque returned from a day in the forest without any birds. Xmucane was very angry with them. "Where are the birds? Why have you returned empty-handed?" she said.

"The birds flew up into the top branches of the tree, Grandmother," said the twins. "They flew so high we could not catch them. We need help to catch them. We want One Monkey and One Artisan to help us." They said this because Hunahpu and Xbalanque had come up with a plan to defeat their envious brothers.

They did not plan to kill One Monkey or One Artisan, but rather to transform them, as a punishment for their envy and the poor treatment they dealt to Hunahpu and Xbalanque. "They did not treat us as brothers," said the twins. "They treated us as slaves, and so we will have justice for that."

And so it was that One Monkey and One Artisan went into the forest with their brothers to hunt birds. They came to a big tree that was full of birds. The birds sat in the branches of the tree and sang. Hunahpu and Xbalanque pointed their blowguns into the trees and shot at the birds, but none of the birds they shot fell to the ground.

"See? This is the problem," said Hunahpu and Xbalanque. "We shoot the birds, but the tree is so large that they get stuck in the branches. We need you to climb the tree and bring the dead birds down to us."

"Very well," said One Monkey and One Artisan, and they began to climb the tree.

Up, up, up they climbed, high among the branches. Then something strange happened. The higher they climbed, the larger the tree became, until the tree was so big that when One Monkey and One Artisan were ready to descend, they could not get down.

"Help us!" cried One Monkey and One Artisan. "Help us, brothers! This tree is frighteningly tall! We cannot get down!"

"Take off your loincloths," said Hunahpu and Xbalanque. "Tie them around your waists, and let the long part dangle behind you. Pull on that loose part. Then you will find that you can climb the trees very well indeed."

One Monkey and One Artisan did as their brothers said. They retied their loincloths, and pulled on the loose end that was dangling behind. As they pulled, the end of their loincloth turned into a tail. Fur began to grow all over their bodies. Their hands and feet became long and slender. Their toes became long and grasping-like fingers.

Their arms became long, and their bodies and heads shrank. One Monkey and One Artisan had become spider monkeys!

One Monkey and One Artisan screamed and chattered, as they no longer had human speech. But climbing trees was not difficult for them: they darted up and down the great tree, climbing with quickness and skill, and swinging from the branches on their tails. They went into the forest, where they climbed about in the trees, screeching at one another.

Hunahpu and Xbalanque went home. When Xmucane saw that their brothers were not with them, she asked what had become of them.

"Never fear, Grandmother," said the twins. "Our brothers are quite safe. In fact, you will see them very soon, but you must promise not to laugh at them. We will call them now. Remember: you must not laugh!"

Hunahpu and Xbalanque took up the flute and the drum. They started playing a song, and the name of the song was "Hunahpu Spider Monkey." One Monkey and One Artisan heard the song where they were out in the forest. They could not resist its call. They came ambling into Grandmother Xmucane's house, chattering and gesturing in the way monkeys do. When Xmucane saw them, she immediately began to laugh. This frightened the monkeys, and they ran back into the forest.

Hunahpu and Xbalanque said, "Shall we try again, Grandmother? We can call them again, but we can only do it four times. We can call them three more times, but you must promise not to laugh."

Xmucane promised not to laugh, so once again Hunahpu and Xbalanque played their song. Once again, One Monkey and One Artisan came into Xmucane's house. They danced about, and they were completely naked in the way of monkeys. Xmucane looked upon their nakedness and their silly dancing. She tried very hard not to laugh, but she could not contain herself. Soon she was laughing very hard indeed, and the two monkeys ran away back into the forest.

The twins tried once more to call their brothers back from the forest. Again, they warned their grandmother not to laugh. Again, the monkeys came when they heard the call of the song, and they danced about in Xmucane's house. This time Xmucane tried even harder not to laugh, but so amusing were the antics of her grandsons that she could not help herself. Yet again she burst out laughing, and the monkeys ran away back into the forest.

"We will try once more, Grandmother," said the twins. And so, they began playing their song, but this time the monkeys did not come. They stayed in the forest instead.

"Do not grieve, Grandmother," said Hunahpu and Xbalanque. "We cannot bring One Monkey and One Artisan back, but we are here. We are here, and we also are your grandsons, and we ask that you love our mother. Know also that we never will forget our brothers. Always will their names be spoken. Always shall we remember their deeds."

And so it came to pass that whenever musicians or writers or carvers began a piece of work, they called upon One Monkey and One Artisan to bless their art. But even though these brothers were revered, they were not considered gods. They did not have that honor, for although their deeds as musicians and writers were good and worthy of memory, they had too much pride and envy, and for those sins they were changed into monkeys.

Now that One Monkey and One Artisan lived in the forest as monkeys, they could not help their family by working in the maize field any longer. "Never fear," said Hunahpu and Xbalanque to their mother and grandmother. "We will do that work now. We will take the place of One Monkey and One Artisan."

The twins took up their farming tools and their blowguns and made ready to go to the maize field. "Bring us a meal at midday please, Grandmother," they said.

"I will bring it," said Xmucane.

The twins arrived at the maize field. They took the hoe and swung it with great strength into the soil. The hoe began to dig furrows in the soil by itself. They took the ax and swung it with great strength into a tree. Then the axe cut down the tree by itself. And so, the hoe plowed the field and dug out the briars from it by itself, and the axe cut down trees.

Hunahpu and Xbalanque saw Turtle Dove at the edge of the field. "Turtle Dove," they said to the bird, "you must be our lookout. When you see Grandmother Xmucane coming, call out to us so that we may take up our tools in our own hands."

Turtle Dove agreed, and went to a place where she could watch for Xmucane. Meanwhile, the twins took their blowguns and went hunting for birds to eat instead of working in the maize field. Soon enough, Turtle Dove called out to the twins. They rubbed dirt all over their bodies. They picked up the hoe and the ax. They pretended to be exhausted from all their hard work. Grandmother came and saw all the work that had been done. She gave the boys their meal, but they had not earned it, for they had not done the work themselves.

Every evening, the twins would return home and pretend to be sore and exhausted from all their work. "Oh!" they said, "Oh, how our backs ache! Oh, how tired our limbs are! Truly we worked very hard today."

Every morning, Hunahpu and Xbalanque went back to the maize field. But when they arrived there, they stopped and stared in wonder. For in the night, all the furrows had been flattened out. All the briars and bushes that had been dug out were back in their places. All the trees that had been chopped down were whole again.

"How has this happened?" cried the twins. "Someone is playing tricks on us."

Now, this is what had happened: in the night, the animals came. They smoothed over the furrows. They replanted the briars and bushes. They made the chopped trees whole. And so it was that when

Hunahpu and Xbalanque arrived the next morning, all their work had been undone.

Again, Hunahpu and Xbalanque plowed furrows and dug out briars and cut down trees. But when the day's work was done, they swore to watch over their field in the night to see who it was that was undoing all their labor. They went home and told their grandmother what had happened and what they planned to do, and so they returned to the maize field to keep watch.

Night fell. Hunahpu and Xbalanque concealed themselves in a place where they could see the field but not be seen themselves. Soon there was a rustling from the forest. Out of the forest poured all manner of animals: jaguars and coyotes, rabbits and deer, tapirs and coatis, and all manner of birds. The animals went to the briars and bushes and bid them replant themselves, and once again the briars and bushes grew in their places. They did the same to the trees, and the trees once again were whole and growing in their places.

Hunahpu and Xbalanque saw the animals undoing all their work. They came out of their concealment and tried to catch the animals. First, they tried to catch jaguar and coyote, but those animals were too quick. Then they tried to catch rabbit and deer. They caught rabbit and deer by their long tails, but the tails broke off, and the animals got away. This is why rabbits and deer have short tails today.

The twins tried and tried to catch the animals, but they had no success. Finally, they were able to catch a rat. They took out their fury on the rat. They held it over the fire and burned the fur off its tail, and this is why rats have naked tails today.

"Stop!" said the rat. "You must not kill me. I have a message for you, and it is this: you are not meant to be maize farmers. But I do know what it is you are meant to do."

"Tell us," said the twins.

"I will tell you if you let me go, and if you give me a little food." said the rat. "I swear that I will not run away and that I will tell you the truth."

"We will give you food after you give us your message," said the twins.

"As you wish," said the rat. "This is my tale: I know where the gaming equipment is, the pads and helmets and ball that belonged to your fathers, One Hunahpu and Seven Hunahpu, who went to Xibalba and died there. If you look in the roof loft of your grandmother's house, there you will find all their equipment for the ballgame. Your grandmother hid these things from you, because your fathers died after accepting a challenge to a ballgame from the Lords of Xibalba."

The twins rejoiced to hear what the rat told them. Then they gave the rat much good food, as they had promised. They gave it maize and chiles and cacao, and many other good things besides. They told the rat that from then on it would have the right to take any morsels of food that had been swept outside the house.

"Now we will take you home with us so you can show us where the ballgame equipment is," said the twins.

"Gladly," said the rat, "but what if your grandmother catches us? What shall we do then?"

"Never fear," said the twins. "We know what to do. We will put you up among the rafters, and you will show us where the things are. We will be able to see what you do reflected in the chile sauce grandmother will make for us."

Then the twins and the rat passed the rest of the night making their plans, and at the noontide they returned home. They hid the rat so that it could not be seen. When they arrived at Grandmother Xmucane's house, one twin went inside while the other went around the outside of the house to put the rat in a place where it could get into the roof loft, and then that twin went inside as well.

"Will you make us some food, Mother?" asked the twins.

"Yes, gladly," said their mother. "What would you like?"

"Oh, make something with that chile sauce that is so very good," they said.

Soon the food was set before them, along with a bowl of chile sauce. The twins pretended to be very thirsty. They drank up all the water in the water jug.

"Will you fetch us some more water, O Grandmother?" they asked. But they were not truly thirsty; this was but a ruse to get the grandmother to leave the room.

While this was going on, the rat waited in the rafters of the house. When the grandmother had left, the rat went to where the ballgame things were. It stood beside the ballgame things, and the twins saw its reflection in the bowl of chile sauce. In this way, Hunahpu and Xbalanque learned where the ballgame equipment had been hidden.

In order to get the equipment down secretly, they also had to send their mother from the house. They told a small biting fly to find the grandmother and to pierce a hole in the water jug so that it would leak. The grandmother did not see the fly, but she did see the leak. She tried and tried to fix it, but she could not.

Back at the house, the twins began to complain about how thirsty they were. "What is taking Grandmother so long? Something surely must have gone wrong. O Mother, go find Grandmother and see whether she needs help."

And so, the mother also left the house, and once she was gone, the rat gnawed through the ropes that were tying the ballgame things in place up in the roof loft. The boys caught the things as they fell, and then went to hide them on the road near the ballcourt. Carrying their blowguns, they next went to the river, where they found the women struggling with the pierced jug.

"What has been taking so long?" asked the twins. "We became impatient with waiting."

"The jug has a hole in it," said the grandmother. "We have been trying to fix it so that we could bring back the water."

Hunahpu and Xbalanque fixed the hole in the jug. And so, the twins and their mother and grandmother returned to the house together.

*Ballgames in Xibalba*

Now that Hunahpu and Xbalanque had the gaming equipment of their fathers, they went to the ballcourt to play. First, they had to clear the field, for it had become overgrown with brush in the time since One Hunahpu and Seven Hunahpu had gone to Xibalba. When the field was clear, they put on their pads and helmets. They took up the ball and began to play. They ran about happily, hitting the ball back and forth and shouting to one another.

The sound of their play resounded below in the halls of Xibalba. The Lords of Death said, "Who is this, making all that racket? Did we not kill One Hunahpu and Seven Hunahpu already? Who could it be, bumping and thumping about?"

The Lords of Death called to the Owl messengers. "Go to those noisy people up there. Tell them that if they wish to play the ballgame, they must come and do it down here. They must come here, with their gaming equipment, in seven days' time, and play the game with us. The Lords of Xibalba command it."

The Owl messengers flew to the house of Xmucane. The Owls told her that in seven days, Hunahpu and Xbalanque must go to Xibalba with their gaming things to play against the Lords of Death.

"I will give them this message," said Xmucane.

When the Owls had left, Xmucane began to weep. She remembered how her sons had been summoned in the same way, and how they had never returned. She did not want to lose her grandsons also. As she wept, a louse fell onto her head. She scratched at it, and then picked it up.

"Little louse," said Xmucane, "I have a message to be taken to my grandsons, who are playing at the ballcourt. Will you take it for me?"

The louse agreed, and scuttled off on its errand. On the road to the ballcourt, there was a toad. The toad saw the louse scuttling along and said, "Where are you going?"

"I am going to the ballcourt," said the louse. "I have a message for the twins."

"Hm," said the toad. "You do not move very quickly. Perhaps it would be better if I swallowed you. I can hop faster than you can scuttle. I will help you take the message."

The louse agreed to this. The toad stuck out its long, sticky tongue. It swallowed the louse, and then went hopping along the road. Presently the toad hopped past a snake.

"Where are you going?" said the snake.

"I am taking a message to the boys who are playing ball at the ballcourt."

"Hm," said the snake. "You do not hop very quickly. Perhaps it would be better if I swallowed you. I can slither faster than you can hop. I will help you take the message."

The toad agreed to this, and presently the snake was slithering along the road, with the toad in its belly. Presently the snake met a falcon, who swallowed the snake. Then the falcon flew swiftly to the ballcourt and alighted on the wall. Hunahpu and Xbalanque were playing ball, but they stopped when they heard the falcon's cry.

"Look! There is a falcon there!" they said. "Let's get our blowguns."

The twins fetched their blowguns. They shot the falcon, hitting him in the eye. The falcon fell from the wall, and the twins picked him up.

"What were you doing there on the wall?" asked the twins.

"I came with a message for you, but I won't tell it until you cure my eye," said the falcon.

The boys agreed to this. They took a small piece of their rubber ball and put it into the eye socket of the falcon. Then the falcon was cured.

"Tell us the message!" said the twins to the falcon, so the falcon vomited up the snake.

"Tell us the message!" said the twins to the snake, so the snake vomited up the toad.

"Tell us the message!" said the twins to the toad, but no matter how he tried, the toad could not vomit up the louse.

"We think you are a liar," said Hunahpu and Xbalanque. They tried to force the toad to vomit, but still he could not vomit up the louse.

Then the boys pried the mouth of the toad open, and there they found the louse. The louse had not been swallowed by the toad. It was just sitting there inside the toad's mouth.

"Tell us the message!" the twins said to the louse.

The louse said, "The Lords of Death bid you come to Xibalba to play the ballgame in seven days' time. You must bring all your own gaming equipment. Your grandmother bade me bring you this message, and because of it, she weeps very sorely."

Hunahpu and Xbalanque let the louse go on its way, and they returned home. There they found Xmucane and their mother, weeping.

"Never fear, Grandmother. Never fear, Mother. We know what we must do," said the twins.

Hunahpu and Xbalanque each planted an ear of maize in the center of the house. They told Xmucane and Lady Blood that if the ears withered, that meant they had died. But if the ears flourished, that meant they were alive.

Then the twins took up their gaming things. They took up their blowguns. Together they took the road that leads to Xibalba. They crossed all the evil rivers, but they did not come to harm. When they arrived at the crossroads, Hunahpu took a hair from his leg and turned it into a mosquito.

"Go to the Lords of Xibalba," the twins said to the mosquito. "Bite them, and listen to what they have to say. Then come and tell us what you heard."

The mosquito buzzed away to the chamber where the Lords of Xibalba were seated. There he found the two wooden figures. He tried biting each of them, but they were only wood. Then he went into the chamber, where he bit One Death.

"Ouch!" said One Death.

"What is it, One Death?" said the others.

"Something bit me!" said One Death.

Then the mosquito went to Seven Death, and bit him too.

"Ouch!" said Seven Death.

"What is it, Seven Death?" said the others.

"Something bit me, too!" said Seven Death.

And in this way, the mosquito bit all the Lords of Death, and thus he learned all their names. But this was no ordinary mosquito, for it had been made from a hair from Hunahpu's leg, and thus the twins heard everything the mosquito had heard. Now the twins knew the names of all the Lords of Xibalba.

Hunahpu and Xbalanque went along the black road. They came to the doorway where the effigies were.

"Greet these lords correctly," said a voice.

But Hunahpu and Xbalanque merely laughed. "These are not lords. They are only wooden figures," they said.

Then the twins went into the chamber where the Lords of Xibalba were seated. Hunahpu and Xbalanque greeted each one of them by name.

The Lords of Xibalba said, "Sit there on that bench."

But Hunahpu and Xbalanque did not sit. They saw that the stone of the bench was heated.

"Go into that house," said the Lords of Xibalba. "Spend the night there, and in the morning, we will play the ballgame."

Messengers guided Hunahpu and Xbalanque to the house, which was the House of Darkness. The messenger of One Death gave each of them an unlit torch and a lit cigar.

"Take these things into the house with you," said the messenger. "Light the torches so that you can see, but be sure to give everything back in the morning, exactly as it is now."

Hunahpu and Xbalanque did not light the torches. Instead, they put some bright red feathers on the ends, to make it look like flames. Then they put out the cigars, but not before they summoned some fireflies. They put the fireflies on the ends of the cigars. And thus it was that the Xibalbans thought that the twins had lit the torches and were smoking the cigars. The Xibalbans watched them all night, and they rejoiced because they were sure that the twins had been defeated.

In the morning, Hunahpu and Xbalanque returned the torches to the lords, unburnt, and the cigars, unsmoked. The Xibalbans were amazed. "Who are they? Who are their parents? Where do they come from? This seems unlikely to end well for us," they said.

Then the boys were summoned before the Lords of Xibalba. "Who are you, and where do you come from?" asked One Death and Seven Death.

63

"Oh, we have no idea where we are from," said the twins.

Then the Xibalbans said, "Let us go to the ballcourt and play ball. We will use our ball for the game."

"No," said Hunahpu and Xbalanque. "We will use our ball."

"Our ball is better," said the Xibalbans. "We will use this one."

"That isn't a ball," said the twins. "It is a skull."

"No, it isn't," said the Xibalbans. "It only looks that way. It's a ball with a skull drawn on it."

"All right, we'll use your ball," said the twins.

And so, the ballgame began. But when the ball made its first bounce a dagger came out of it. The ball bounced around the court, trying to slash the twins with the dagger.

"Is that any way to treat your guests?" said the twins. "You invited us here to play the ballgame, but now you are trying to kill us. Very well; we will just go home now. We will not play."

"No, please don't leave," said the Xibalbans. "Stay and play. We will use your ball."

Hunahpu and Xbalanque agreed to stay. "What shall we have as our wager?" they asked.

"If we win, you must bring us four bowls of flowers," said the Lords of Death, "some with whole blossoms and some with just the petals."

"That is a fair wager," said the twins. "Let us play."

And so, the game began. Up and down the court the players ran. It was a hard-fought game, and the twins played well, but in the end the Xibalbans won.

"You will bring us the wager in the morning," said the Lords of Death. "And then we will play ball again."

Messengers took Hunahpu and Xbalanque to the House of Knives, where they were to spend the night. The twins could hear the blades of the knives clashing against one another. When they entered the house, the twins said, "Do not cut us. Cut the flesh of animals instead."

When they said that, the knives ceased their clashing. The knives did not cut Hunahpu and Xbalanque. Then the twins called to the ants. "Ants! Leaf-cutters! Come to our aid! Come and help us! Collect up flower petals and flower blossoms, four bowls full."

The ants agreed to help the twins. They went into the garden, and began to collect flower petals.

Now, the Lords of Xibalba had set some birds to act as watchmen. They told the birds, "Allow no one into the garden! No one at all!"

The birds agreed to watch the garden, but they did not see the ants. They just flitted about in the trees and bushes, singing their night songs. The ants climbed up into the plants and cut down flower petals. They cut down blossoms. They even climbed up onto the birds and clipped off some of their feathers, but the birds did not notice. The ants worked all night, collecting flower petals and whole blossoms, and soon they had filled four bowls.

In the morning, a messenger was sent to the House of Knives to bring Hunahpu and Xbalanque before the Lords of Xibalba. The twins went into the chamber where the Lords sat, bearing the four bowls of flower petals and whole blossoms. The Lords of Xibalba saw the bowls full of flower petals and whole blossoms, and they knew they had been defeated. They called to themselves the bird guardians and said, "Explain yourselves! We told you to guard our flowers, but here we have four bowls full of flower petals and whole blossoms."

"We do not know what happened," said the birds, "but even we were attacked. Look at our tails!" And they showed their tails to the Lords, their tails with the feathers the ants had plucked out.

The Lords of Xibalba were very angry with the bird guardians, and as punishment, they split the birds' mouths wide open.

Then the Lords went to play ball again with the twins, but nobody won that match.

"We will play again in the morning," said the Lords.

"Yes," said the twins, "we will gladly play again tomorrow."

That night the Xibalbans put Hunahpu and Xbalanque in the House of Ice. It was incredibly cold inside the house. The twins' breath misted thickly before their faces. Hail rained down on them. Hail covered the floor of the house, and the walls and rafters were thick with ice. Hunahpu and Xbalanque worked quickly. They built a fire of good logs and stood before it all night.

When the Xibalbans went to fetch the twins in the morning they said to themselves, "Ha! There is no way they could have survived the House of Ice! When we open the door, we will see their dead bodies, and we will have victory!"

But when they opened the door, they did not see the dead bodies of the twins. Instead, they saw Hunahpu and Xbalanque standing there, perfectly well and alive. "Good morning," said the twins. "Shall we go to the ballcourt and play?"

At the end of that day, the Xibalbans put the twins in the House of Jaguars. "Surely they will never survive this night," said the Xibalbans to themselves.

The House of Jaguars was full of hungry jaguars. The fierce cats surrounded the twins, growling and prowling. Hunahpu and Xbalanque said, "Do not bite us, O Jaguars! Here are bones for you to gnaw!"

And so, the twins threw bones to the jaguars, and the cats gnawed on those instead.

Outside the house, the Xibalbans heard the noise of crunching bones. "Ha!" they said to themselves. "The jaguars are eating those two for sure. We will find nothing left of them at all when we open the door in the morning."

Again, the Xibalbans were disappointed, for when they opened the door of the House of Jaguars, they found Hunahpu and Xbalanque perfectly well and alive.

The next night, the Lords of Xibalba put the twins in the House of Fire, but they were not burned at all. In the morning, Hunahpu and Xbalanque came out of the house perfectly well and alive.

The night after that, the twins were put in the House of Bats. But these were no ordinary bats: they were great Death Bats, and anyone who went near them was instantly killed. Hunahpu and Xbalanque crawled inside their blowguns to escape the Death Bats, and there they were safe.

All night long, the twins listened to the cries of the bats and to the flapping of their great wings. The bats made a great din, all night long. But after a time, the noise died down.

"Is it morning yet?" asked Xbalanque. "Are the bats asleep?"

"I don't know," said Hunahpu. "I'll go look."

Hunahpu crawled to the end of his blowgun. He stuck his head out the end to see whether it was morning. Suddenly, a great Death Bat swooped down and cut off Hunahpu's head.

Xbalanque waited inside his blowgun, but when no word came after a time, he said, "Hunahpu? Is it morning yet?"

But no answer came.

Xbalanque asked again, "Is it morning? What do you see?"

But no answer came save some light fluttering of bats' wings. And it was then that Xbalanque knew that they had been defeated, and that his brother was dead.

The Xibalbans celebrated the death of Hunahpu. One Death and Seven Death said, "Let his head be put atop the ballcourt!" And so that was done.

Meanwhile, from inside his blowgun, Xbalanque called to the animals. "Animals! O Animals great and small! Come to me; come and get your food."

And so, the animals came to where Xbalanque was, looking for their food. Last of all came a turtle. He came slowly and calmly, as is the way of turtles. The turtle walked over to the body of Hunahpu. It attached itself to Hunahpu's neck, and so a new head began to be fashioned. Heart of Sky came down into the House of Bats to help make a new head for Hunahpu.

All night long they worked to make a new head, but soon dawn was approaching, and the only thing that had been finished was the outside. Xbalanque called to the vulture. "Old One!" cried Xbalanque. "Make it dark again."

"I will do this," said the vulture, and immediately it became dark.

And so, the darkness lasted until Hunahpu's new head was completely finished, and then the dawn broke in the eastern sky. Then Hunahpu and Xbalanque took counsel together. They planned what they were going to do. "The Lords will want to play ball again," said Xbalanque. "You hang back; let me do all the playing." Then Xbalanque called to himself a rabbit. "O Rabbit," he said, "go and hide over there near the ballcourt. When I hit the ball toward you, bound across the ballcourt."

The rabbit went to the place he was to hide. Xbalanque and Hunahpu went to the ballcourt. When the Xibalbans saw Hunahpu, they said, "Ha! We have already defeated you. We don't know why you have even bothered coming here. Maybe we should hit your head with the ball!"

This made Hunahpu very angry, but he gave them no answer. And so, they began their ballgame. They played up and down the court, but Hunahpu hung back and did very little. Xbalanque played for both of them instead. After a time, the Xibalbans hit the ball toward the hoop. Xbalanque blocked the shot, and sent the ball bouncing toward the place where the rabbit was hiding. When the ball arrived there, the rabbit came bounding across the ballcourt as Xbalanque had asked him to do. The rabbit bounded and bounced just like the ball, and so the Xibalbans went running after the rabbit.

While the Xibalbans were chasing the rabbit, the twins ran over to the place where Hunahpu's real head was. They took that head down and replaced it with the head that had been made out of the turtle. They put Hunahpu's real head back on his body, and he was made whole. Laughing for joy, the twins went to the place where the real ball was. They brought it back to the ballcourt. They called to the Lords of Xibalba saying, "Look! We have the ball here. Let us finish our game."

The Lords came back, and they played ball with the twins. Now that Hunahpu had his own head back, he could play properly again. Back and forth and up and down the court the twins went, playing hard against the Xibalbans. No matter how hard the Xibalbans tried, they could not defeat the twins. The game ended in a tie. At the very end, Xbalanque threw the ball at the false head of Hunahpu where it sat atop the ballcourt. The head toppled from the wall, and split apart when it hit the ground.

"What is that?" said the Lords of Xibalba. "Who put that there?"

And so it was that Hunahpu and Xbalanque defeated the Lords of Xibalba. The Lords put the twins through many trials, but every time Hunahpu and Xbalanque defeated them and did not die.


*The Deaths and Resurrections of Hunahpu and Xbalanque*

Even though Hunahpu and Xbalanque had been through many trials, they knew there was no way the Xibalbans would let them leave alive. And so, the twins called to themselves two wise soothsayers, to give instructions about what to do with their bodies.

The twins said, "The Xibalbans will surely kill us; we will not leave here alive. We think that they will burn us. This is what you are to say when they ask what to do with our bones. Tell them not to throw the bones into the canyon; we will come back to life if they do that. Tell them not to hang our bones in the trees; that will merely remind them of all the times we defeated them. Tell them to scatter our bones in the river, but that first they should grind the bones into powder. They should grind our bones well, like the finest maize flour, and then pour that into the river."

"We will do as you say," said the soothsayers.

While the twins were speaking with the soothsayers, the Lords of Xibalba were making a huge bonfire. They were making it to kill Hunahpu and Xbalanque. When the fire was all made and very hot, the Xibalbans came to fetch the twins. "Let us play a game with the fire!" said One Death and Seven Death. "Let us fly across it, and see who comes out alive!"

But the twins were not fooled by this. "We know you mean to kill us," they said, "so let us finish that task right now."

And so, the twins embraced one another, and then jumped into the bonfire, where they died. The Xibalbans celebrated the deaths of Hunahpu and Xbalanque. They sang and danced. They jumped and shouted. And when their celebration was done, they sent for the soothsayers.

"What shall we do with their bones?" asked the Xibalbans.

"Grind them into powder, grind them like the finest maize flour, and then pour that into the river," said the soothsayers.

The Xibalbans ground the bones into powder. They poured the powder into the river. The powder floated away down the river, but soon it began to sink to the bottom. There on the bottom of the river the powder gathered up. It gathered itself, and made itself into two boys. It made itself into two beautiful boys, and Hunahpu and Xbalanque were alive again.

After five days, they came out of the river and began to show themselves to the people, but to the people they did not look like beautiful boys: they looked like fish people. When the Xibalbans learned that the twins were alive again, they began to search for them in all the rivers, but they did not find them.

Then the twins dressed themselves in rags. They went about pretending to be orphans. Wherever they went, they performed dances and worked miracles. They burned down houses and then made them whole, as though nothing had ever happened. One of them would kill the other, and then bring him back to life. The Xibalbans watched all of this, marveling at the deeds of these strange orphans. The Xibalbans watched, not knowing that in this way the twins were planting the seeds of their victory over the Lords of Death.

Soon enough, word of their skillful dancing came to the ears of One Death and Seven Death. They called to themselves their messengers. "Go and fetch these orphans," said One Death and Seven Death. "Tell them we command them to come before us and perform their dances and work their miracles. We have heard of their skill and wish to see it for ourselves."

The messengers went to Hunahpu and Xbalanque. They delivered the message of One Death and Seven Death. But the twins refused to go. "We do not wish to dance before the Lords of Death," they said. "We are but poor orphans. We do not belong in a stately house such as theirs. It is better if we do not go."

The messengers insisted that the twins should go. The messengers bullied them and threatened them. Finally, the twins agreed to go, but they went very, very slowly, with a great show of reluctance.

Finally, Hunahpu and Xbalanque arrived in the chamber of One Death and Seven Death, where they sat with the other Lords of

Xibalba. The twins prostrated themselves in front of the Lords. They bowed low, they behaved in the most humblest of ways.

"Who are your people?" asked the Lords. "Where do you come from?"

"We are just poor orphans," replied the twins. "We have never known our parents. We don't know where we come from."

"It does not matter, then," said the Lords. "Perform your dances and miracles now. We will pay you when you are done."

"Oh, we require no payment, Lords," said the twins. "This place is very frightening. We are frightened indeed."

"Never fear," said One Death and Seven Death. "Perform your dances and miracles. Do the dances. Work the miracle where you make a sacrifice and then bring him back to life. Burn down our house and then restore it. Show us all the wonders you can do, and you will be handsomely rewarded."

And so, the twins began their dancing. They did the Armadillo Dance. They did the Weasel Dance. They did the Owl Dance, and many other dances. The Xibalbans watched them with great wonder and delight, for Hunahpu and Xbalanque were skilled dancers indeed.

"Now do the sacrifice trick," said One Death. "Cut up my dog and bring him back to life again."

The twins sacrificed the dog. They cut the dog into pieces, and then brought it back to life again. When the dog came back to life, it was very happy and went about wagging its tail.

"Now burn down my house," said One Death. "Burn down my house and restore it again."

Hunahpu and Xbalanque burned the house down. They burned it down with all the Lords inside it, but no one was harmed. They burned the house down and then restored it, as though nothing had ever happened. The Xibalbans marveled at this. They were much delighted by the miracle of the burning house that was restored.

Next the Lords demanded that the twins sacrifice a person and revive him. The twins took a person and cut out his heart. They took the heart and showed it to the Lords. Then they brought the person back to life again, and he was very happy to have his life restored to him.

"That is most marvelous!" cried the Lords. "Now sacrifice each other. Do that one, where you sacrifice each other and come back to life again."

"Very well," said the twins, and so Xbalanque sacrificed Hunahpu. Xbalanque cut his brother's body into pieces. The Lords of Xibalba watched this with great delight. Then Xbalanque brought Hunahpu back to life, and the Lords were even more happy and amazed.

"Oh!" said One Death and Seven Death. "That is a wonder indeed! Now do that to us! Sacrifice us, and bring us back to life!"

"Very well," said the twins. And so, they sacrificed One Death and Seven Death. The twins tore out the hearts of the Lords of Death, but they did not restore them to life. The twins let them stay dead, as punishment for their misdeeds.

A third Lord cowered before Hunahpu and Xbalanque. "Do not kill me!" he cried. "Have mercy!"

But when the other Xibalbans saw what had happened to One Death and Seven Death, they fled, because they were afraid that Hunahpu and Xbalanque would sacrifice them next. They ran and ran. They ran to the lip of a canyon and threw themselves over the edge, thinking that they could hide there. But there were so many of them, that soon the canyon was completely filled with the bodies of the Xibalbans.

Soon the ants discovered the canyon full of bodies. The ants ran into the canyon. They climbed all over the Xibalbans. This drove the Xibalbans out of the canyon. They went before the twins and begged them for mercy.

It was then that Hunahpu and Xbalanque revealed who they truly were. They said their names before the assembled Xibalbans. "We are Hunahpu and Xbalanque," they said, "and we are the sons of One Hunahpu and Seven Hunahpu, who came here to your realm and who were killed by you. We came here to avenge their deaths. We came here, and you put us through many sore trials. For those misdeeds, we shall surely kill you all!"

When the Xibalbans heard this, they all fell to their knees before the twins. "No, no!" they cried. "Do not kill us! Have mercy! Our deeds against your fathers surely were wrong; we confess it. We confess that our deeds against them were evil and that we killed them and buried them near the ballcourt. We are very sorry for that. Have mercy!"

Hunahpu and Xbalanque heard the pleas of the Xibalbans. They heard their cries for mercy and said, "Very well. We will not kill you. But still you must be punished. Never again will you receive good offerings. Yours will be croton sap, not fresh blood. Never shall you have offerings of sound goods, but only those that are cracked and worn. Never again will you be able to take good people. Only those who have truly done wrong will be for you."

And so it was that the Lords of Xibalba lost their status. They became lowered in their rank. They had never been gods, but still people had honored them. But after the coming of Hunahpu and Xbalanque to Xibalba, they were made unworthy of honor or worship. They were unworthy because they were untruthful and unfaithful, because they had bad hearts. Hunahpu and Xbalanque humbled the Lords of Xibalba. They took away their rank and status from them.

Now, while Hunahpu and Xbalanque were in Xibalba, their grandmother Xmucane had watched the ears of maize the twins had planted within the house. For many days, the maize was green and growing, but when Hunahpu and Xbalanque jumped into the bonfire, the maize withered and died. Xmucane saw that the twins had died, and she mourned greatly. She shed many bitter tears and burned incense before the maize, in memory of her grandsons. But then the boys came back to life, and so did the maize. Xmucane saw this and rejoiced. She celebrated when the maize came back to life.

Xmucane worshiped the reborn maize plants. She gave them a new name. She called them "Center of the House" and "Green Reeds." Thus did Xmucane honor her grandsons. Thus did she honor their memory.

After Hunahpu and Xbalanque defeated the Lords of Xibalba, they sought out the place where One Hunahpu and Seven Hunahpu had been buried. They went looking for the pieces of One Hunahpu's body. They found many of the pieces, but they could not make him whole. They found One Hunahpu's head, but when asked to say its name, it could not.

When the twins found that they could not restore their father to life, they said, "Be comforted, father. Be comforted, uncle. Your name shall not be forgotten. The name of Hunahpu will belong always to this place.

"We have avenged your deaths. We have avenged all the misdeeds committed against you by the Lords of Xibalba. May your hearts be at peace."

Then Hunahpu and Xbalanque rose into the heavens. Up, up, up they rose, high in the sky. One became the sun, and the other became the moon. They dwelled together in the sky ever after.

With them arose the four hundred boys who had been killed by Zipacna. The four hundred boys rose up into the sky with Hunahpu and Xbalanque, and there they became a constellation.

And this is the end of the tale of Hunahpu and Xbalanque, and of all their deeds, and of their transformation when their deeds were accomplished.

# PART III: THREE MAYA FOLKTALES

## The Man Who Became a Buzzard

*This story of a lazy man who is changed into a buzzard exists in multiple variants throughout Central America. In some stories, the man is permanently changed, while in others he is allowed to resume his human form. Whatever their ending, each of these stories is a cautionary tale about the value of hard work and of accepting one's place in the world. In this retelling, I am following the ending related by Martha Schmitt in her collection of Central American legends.*

Once there was a farmer who lived together with his wife, and they were very poor indeed. The reason they were so poor was that the husband was extremely lazy. Every day he would go out to his fields, but instead of working hard caring for his crops and clearing land, he would do only a little work in the morning and then for the rest of the day he would sit under a shady tree and take a nap, or he would go to the river and paddle about in the water, or he would lie on his back and watch the clouds floating by in the sky. And so, his crops never grew well, and he never had space to plant more, because he did not do his work.

One day, as the man lay on his back gazing at the sky, he saw a buzzard sailing in slow circles in the air above him. "What a life!" said the man to himself. "What a life it must be, to just sail through the air like that, and to never have to work. I wish I could be like that buzzard. Then I would be content indeed."

Then the man had an idea.

"Hey!" he shouted at the buzzard. "Hey! Come down here and talk to me!"

The buzzard flew in slow circles above the man. He flew, circling and circling, and the man began to think that maybe the buzzard hadn't heard him. But then the buzzard began to descend, ever circling, until finally he landed in the field next to the man.

"What do you want?" croaked the buzzard.

"I have an idea for you," said the man. "I've watched you circling up there in the sky, without a care in the world, while meanwhile I have to work so hard down here on the ground. And so, I have an idea for you. How about we change places? I could put on your feathers and fly about, and you could put on my clothes and work my farm."

"Well," said the bird, "being a buzzard might not be as good as you think it is. Yes, we fly about, but that's because we're looking for food. We eat dead animals, you know. Ones that are dead and rotting. The more rotten the better. That's what you'd have to eat."

"Yes, I know that," said the man. "I know buzzards eat rotten meat. I think I could do that, if it meant I didn't have to work anymore. If you changed places with me, you could eat the good food my wife cooks. Our food is very simple, and we don't have much, but she cooks it well."

The buzzard thought for a moment, then he said, "All right. I will change places with you. Give me your clothes and skin and I will give you my feathers."

The man took off his clothes and skin and gave them to the buzzard. The buzzard took off his feathers and gave them to the man. And soon there in the field stood a buzzard and a man, but they had changed places. The man in the buzzard's feathers flapped away up into the sky and flew in two circles above the field, then he returned to the ground.

"Right!" said the man, who had become a buzzard. "I am a buzzard now. I like my wings. Thank you for trading with me! Now, let me show you where my house is, so that you can meet my wife. I'll alight on the roof, and you will know that that is my house."

The man flapped his new wings and went flying into the sky. The buzzard moved his new legs and walked. Together they went to the man's house, where the man who had become a buzzard alighted on the roof. Once the buzzard who had become a man knew which house it was, the man flew away. The buzzard in the man's skin went into the man's house. He went to the man's wife to greet her, but she pushed him away. "Oh!" she cried. "Oh, you smell so very, very bad! What have you been doing, that you smell that way?"

"I have been working in the fields," said the buzzard. "It is very hard work, and I am sweating a lot. That's why I smell bad."

"Wait here," said the wife. "I will go and prepare a bath for you."

The wife prepared a sweat bath for the buzzard. The buzzard took off the man's clothes and went into the sweat bath, but he didn't like it much. It was so hot and so damp. He became truly uncomfortable, and so he left the bath and went back into the house, even though he still smelled bad and wasn't clean at all.

Meanwhile, the man in the buzzard's feathers decided to enjoy his new wings. He went up, up, up into the sky and began flying in circles. He was very pleased with being a buzzard. "This is the life!" he said. "This is the way to be, flying in circles, up here in the sky!"

After a time, he began to be hungry. He thought about what he would have to eat as a buzzard, and it made him sick to his stomach.

Even being able to fly about in the sky was not enough to make him want to remain a buzzard if he had to eat dead, rotting animals. He decided to go home. He flew over his house and circled above the roof a few times before landing on the ground outside the door. Then he went into the house. Hop, hop, hop he went, as buzzards do, because he still wore the buzzard's feathers.

He saw the buzzard who was wearing his skin inside the house arguing with his wife.

"You still smell so bad! Didn't you finish your bath?" said the wife.

"No, I didn't. I don't like that bath at all," said the buzzard. "It is too hot and too damp. Anyway, I can't help the way I smell, can I? I've always smelled like this."

Then the wife caught sight of the man who had turned into a buzzard. She screamed when she saw the large, ugly bird standing there in the house.

"Rawk, rawk!" croaked the bird. It was the man, trying to tell his wife that he was her husband, but she didn't understand. Instead, she grabbed a broom and started trying to hit the huge bird.

"Rawk!" croaked the bird, as it tried to hop out of the way of the broom.

"Wait!" said the buzzard who had turned into a man. "Wait! Don't hurt that bird! That is your husband. He and I changed places. He wanted to try being a buzzard, and I wanted to try being a man. That's why I smell so bad."

"Well, change back!" said the woman. "Give him back his skin and clothes, and he'll give you back your feathers."

"We can't change back," said the buzzard. "We have to stay the way we are."

The wife began to cry, because although her husband was very lazy indeed, she still loved him. The man who had become a buzzard was also very sad, because he loved his wife, and although he could still fly about in the sky, now he could only eat rotten meat instead of his wife's good cooking. And although the buzzard who had become a man got to eat the good cooking, he now had to work very, very hard, and take baths whenever his wife told him to.

### How the Sun and Moon Became Man and Wife

*The tropes of the old man who doesn't wish his daughter to marry and of the young couple who must go through a sore trial before they can wed is common to many cultures. In this tale from Guatemala, these tropes are woven into a just-so story that explains the creation of the moon, snakes, and many kinds of insects.*

Long, long ago, when the world was new, there was an old man who lived alone with his only daughter. The daughter was very beautiful, and she was very skilled and industrious. She knew how to spin and weave, she knew how to sew, she knew how to keep a good garden, and how to cook delicious food. She looked after her father very well, and he looked after her, and together they were very happy.

One day, the Sun happened to see the old man's daughter, who was sitting outside spinning some new thread. The Sun looked at her, and fell in love. She was so very beautiful! Her long black hair shone in the light, her dark eyes twinkled with merriment, and her strong fingers worked quickly and well with her spindle and thread. That very moment, the Sun decided that he must have the young woman for his bride.

The Sun decided that he would turn himself into a hunter and impress the young woman with his strength and prowess at the hunt. Surely that way he would win her heart, and they could be wed and live together in great happiness. But there was not much game to be found in the part of the forest where the old man lived with his daughter, so the Sun thought of a way he might trick the young woman into thinking him a fine hunter. He found the skin of a deer, then filled it with ashes and dried grass and sewed it up so that it looked like he had caught a fine, fat animal that would feed a family well. Then he put the false deer on his shoulders, and strode past the old man's house where the daughter sat working at her spindle.

And so, for many days, the Sun took the form of a handsome, strong young man. In the mornings he would walk past the old man's house with his bow and arrows, and in the afternoons, he would return with the fat, false deer on his shoulders, as though he had just killed it and was going home to cook and eat it. Now, the young woman noticed the young man striding by—although she gave no hint to him that she was looking—for he was indeed well to look upon, with his thick, black hair and his warm, brown eyes, and his broad shoulders and his fine, strong legs. Surely he would make a good husband for some lucky woman, as handsome as he was, and as skilled at the hunt, for he never failed to return home with a fat deer.

One morning, after the young man had passed by the old man's house, the daughter went to her father and said, "Father, I think that young hunter would make a good husband for me. He is so very handsome, and he always comes home with a fat deer."

"Hm," said the old man. "I am not sure of that. There is not much game in this part of the forest. He could be tricking you. Young men do that sort of thing, sometimes. Next time he goes past, throw some water onto the ground in front of him. That might tell you something about him."

That afternoon, the young woman sat in front of her father's house washing some maize in a bowl full of water. Soon enough, the young hunter came into view, with the deer on his shoulders. Remembering what her father had said, the young woman put the maize into a different bowl and then threw the water onto the ground in the hunter's path. When his foot touched the wet earth, the hunter slipped and fell. He landed right on top of the false deer, splitting the seams and sending a great cloud of ash into the air. The woman saw this, and gasped. The Sun felt very ashamed, because now his trick was made plain before her, so he changed himself into a hummingbird and flew away.

But even though his trick with the deerskin had gone awry, the Sun still was in love with the beautiful young woman, and he could not stay away from her. In the form of a hummingbird, he would go into the old man's garden and flit amongst the flowers there, and in that way, he would watch the young woman at her work. One day, the young woman noticed the hummingbird flying in the garden and sipping nectar. The bird was such a pretty thing, with bright, shining feathers, that she wanted to have it for her own, and she did not know that this little bird was the Sun in disguise.

The young woman went to her father and said, "Father, will you get your blowgun and catch that hummingbird for me?"

"Certainly, my dear," said the old man, and he went out into the garden and PHUT! he blew a shot at the hummingbird and knocked it to the ground, stunned. The young woman ran to pick up the little-feathered thing. She cradled it carefully in her hands, then took it into the house, where she put it in her room.

That night, while the young woman slept, the Sun turned himself back into the form of a young man. The young woman woke up and found him standing there in her room.

"What are you doing here?" she said. "Who are you? If my father finds you here, he will kill us both!"

"Have no fear," said the man. "I am the young hunter who tried to trick you with the deer, but you were too clever for me. And I am the hummingbird who drank nectar from the flowers in your garden, but your father captured me with his blowgun. I saw you sitting in your father's garden many, many days ago, and I fell in love with you. Come away with me, and be my wife! We will live together most happily, that I promise you."

"Oh!" said the young woman. "I should very much like to go with you, but it is not safe. My father has a magic stone, in which he can see anything he chooses, both far and near. And he has a magic blowgun that he could use to kill us. We would never be able to get away from him."

"Never mind that," said the Sun. "I will make it safe for us; you will see."

Creeping through the house as quietly as two mice, the young man and young woman went to the place where the old man kept his magic stone and his magic blowgun. The Sun took some ash and poured it all over the stone, so that the old man would not be able to see anything in it. Then he took some ground chili powder and put it inside the blowgun. That done, the pair slipped out the door and into the forest.

In the morning, the old man woke and called to his daughter, but she did not answer. He went through the house and garden looking for her, but did not find her. Angry that his daughter had run away, the old man went to the place where he kept his magic stone. He picked it up, and tried to see where the young woman had gone, but he couldn't see through the ash the Sun had poured on it. Suddenly, he saw that there was one spot where there was no ash, because the Sun had not been careful enough in covering the whole stone. In that small spot on the stone, the old man saw his daughter with a young man on the river in a canoe.

The old man trembled with rage. How dare his daughter leave with a young man without his permission! He took up his blowgun and went out after the young couple. He put the blowgun to his lips and drew in a breath so that he could take a shot, but instead of air, he breathed in the ground chili powder. How the old man coughed, and how his eyes watered! How his throat and his mouth burned! The old man was furious. He called to the lightning to go and strike down the young man and his daughter.

The Sun and the young woman were in the canoe, paddling as fast as they could to get away from the old man. The Sun realized that a lightning bolt was coming. "Jump into the water!" he said, and then threw himself into the river, where he turned into a turtle and swam as fast as he could toward the river bottom. The young woman also jumped into the water, where she became a crab. But she couldn't swim as fast as the turtle, so when the lightning bolt struck the water, it hit her.

The young woman's blood slowly spread out over the surface of the water. The Sun swam up from the depths of the river, where he saw the blood of his beloved floating on the surface. The Sun wept with grief. He called to the dragonflies for help, asking them to collect up the blood for him. The dragonflies did as the Sun bid them. They collected up all the blood, putting it into little bottles. When they were finished, they gave the bottles to the Sun, who hid them away in a safe place.

After a certain time, the Sun returned to the place where he had hidden the bottles. He opened the first one, and a great many snakes came pouring out. He opened the second one, and a cloud of wasps buzzed out of it and into the sky. The Sun opened bottle after bottle, and from each one poured a different kind of small creature, that then flew or crawled away. And that is how snakes and many kinds of insects came to be in the world.

Finally, the Sun opened the very last bottle. In that bottle was the young woman, as beautiful as ever, with her long, shining, dark hair, and merry eyes, and skillful fingers. The Sun took her hand and drew her up into the heavens with him, where he could gaze on her beauty and where she could delight in his strength, for when she went up with him, she was transformed into the Moon. And there in the heavens the Sun and the Moon have lived happily as husband and wife ever since.

## Rabbit Gets His Drink

*The rabbit is a trickster in the Maya culture, as he is in many others. In this story from Nicaragua, Rabbit needs to find a way to get to the waterhole safely which, of course, he does by means of a trick.*

As everyone knows, Rabbit is a clever animal. He lives by his wits, always getting into trouble and then getting out of it again. One village had constant problems with Rabbit. He was forever getting into their gardens and stealing their vegetables, and doing other naughty things. The villagers went to the king and said, "We cannot abide Rabbit's tricks any longer. You must rid us of him."

Now, the king was a wise man, and he knew how clever Rabbit was. He also had many other important things to do besides deal with naughty Rabbits. He told the villagers, "Very well. If you catch him and bring him here to me, I will deal with him."

The villagers thought this a fair bargain, so they went home and called a meeting to decide how to catch Rabbit. They thought of traps they might set, but then they remembered that every trap they had tried in the past had failed. Then someone said, "Why don't we lie in wait for him at the waterhole? All the animals go there to drink. Eventually Rabbit will become thirsty, and he will go to the waterhole, too. Then we can grab him while he is taking his drink, and bring him to the king."

The others thought this a splendid plan. They went to the waterhole and hid themselves among the trees and bushes, waiting for Rabbit to come and get his drink. They waited and waited, not knowing that when they had their meeting, Rabbit had been hiding nearby. Rabbit heard everything the villagers said. He knew that the waterhole was not a safe place for him anymore, but he also knew that soon he would be thirsty. Rabbit set to thinking, and soon he had a plan. He would trick the villagers. Then he would be able to drink all the water he wanted. And the villagers would be able to do nothing about it.

First Rabbit went to another village, one where the people did not know him. He went along the street until he came to a shoemaker's shop. The shoemaker was sitting outside his shop, working on a lovely new pair of shoes.

"Good morning!" said Rabbit to the shoemaker. "A fine, hot day, is it not?"

"Good morning!" said the shoemaker. "Yes, it is indeed both fine and very hot."

"Maybe you should go inside," said Rabbit. "I can see that you are a hard worker. You have made so many lovely shoes already today. Why don't you go inside, and get yourself a nice cool drink? You deserve it."

"Why, I do believe I am thirsty," said the shoemaker. "I will do as you suggest."

As soon as the shoemaker was inside, Rabbit selected a pretty pair of red shoes and hopped away with them. Rabbit went down the road for some time. Then he saw a man coming toward him. The man was carrying a heavy gourd on his back, the kind of gourd that people often fill with golden, sweet honey.

"Oh!" said Rabbit to himself. "That gourd is probably full of honey. Sweet honey would be a tasty treat right now, and it's just the thing I need for my trick!"

Rabbit dropped one of the shoes in the middle of the road, then hopped off to the side and hid in some bushes. Soon enough, the man came along and found the single shoe.

"What is this?" said the man, stooping to pick up the shoe. "Why, this is a very pretty shoe, and just the right size for my daughter. Alas, it's only a single shoe, so it does us no good."

The man dropped the shoe in the road where he had found it, and carried on with his journey.

Rabbit was delighted. That was exactly what he wanted the man to do. Rabbit took the remaining shoe and ran with it up the road, ahead of the man. Rabbit put the other shoe in the road where the man would find it, and then hid himself in the bushes again. Sure enough, when the man came upon the shoe, he picked it up and said, "Oh!

This matches the one I saw back there. I shall have a fine pair of shoes to give my daughter now. But first I'll put down my gourd; it's heavy, and there's no reason to carry it back and forth."

And so, the man set his gourd down in the road, and went to get the first shoe.

As soon as the man's back was turned, Rabbit hopped out into the road. He picked up the gourd, and hurried back into the forest. Rabbit ran along, carrying the gourd, until he came to a clearing. The floor of the clearing was covered with fallen leaves.

"Oh!" said Rabbit. "This is a fine place to sit and eat my honey."

Rabbit opened the gourd and began to eat the honey. It was golden, and sweet, and very good. Rabbit ate and ate and ate until he thought he would burst. Even so, there was still quite a bit of honey left, for it was a very large gourd. Rabbit took the remaining honey and poured it all over his body. He poured it into his fur, and down his legs, and up his ears, and even made sure there was some on the puff of his white, fluffy tail. Rabbit was soon covered all over with golden, sticky honey.

Then Rabbit hopped into the middle of the clearing. He flopped down onto the fallen leaves and began to roll, back and forth, back and forth, until he was all covered with fallen leaves. When the leaves touched the honey, there they stuck, and did not fall off. Soon Rabbit looked nothing at all like a rabbit. Not a bit of his fur was visible, not even the puff of his white, fluffy tail. He looked like some kind of odd leaf-creature that hopped out of a dark corner of the forest.

Covered in his leaf disguise, Rabbit went back to his home village. He hopped right down the middle of the main street, but no one recognized him. In fact, the people were a little bit frightened, because they had never seen a creature quite like that before. Piles of leaves and twigs were not supposed to have legs! Piles of leaves and twigs were not supposed to hop down the middle of the street! The people were frightened enough that they did not go near Rabbit at all.

Rabbit hopped down the middle of the main street, right down to the waterhole. The villagers who were lying in wait for Rabbit saw him coming toward them, but they did not recognize him, either. All they saw was a strange leaf-creature, hopping, hopping, hopping toward the water, so they stayed in their hiding places.

Rabbit chuckled to himself as he hopped up to the edge of the water. He knew the villagers were watching him, but they did not recognize him! This was a fine trick he had played, for sure.

Rabbit was thirsty after playing tricks and eating so much honey. He took a long, long drink of water, as much as he liked. Then he hopped away.

The villagers never did catch Rabbit, and they never did bring him before the king.

# Here's another book that I think you'd be interested in:

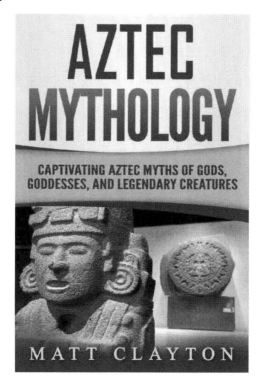

# BIBLIOGRAPHY

Alexander, Harley Burr. *Mythology of All Races.* Vol. 11, *Latin-American.* Boston: Marshall Jones Co., 1920.

Allan, Tony, and Tom Lowenstein. *Gods of Sun & Sacrifice: Aztec & Maya Myth.* London: Duncan Baird Publishers, 1997.

Bierhorst, John. *The Mythology of Mexico and Central America.* Revised edition. Oxford: Oxford University Press, 2002.

————, ed. *The Monkey's Haircut and Other Stories Told by the Maya.* New York: William Morrow and Company, 1986.

Brinton, Daniel G. *American Hero-Myths: A Study in the Native Religions of the Western Continent.* Philadelphia: H. C. Watts & Co., 1882.

Christenson, Allen J., trans. *Popol Vuh: Sacred Book of the Maya People.* 2007. Electronic version of original 2003 publication (Alresford: O Books). Mesoweb: www.mesoweb.com/publications/Christenson/PopolVuh.pdf.

Craine, Eugene R., and Reginald C. Reindorp, trans. and eds. *The Codex Pérez and The Book of Chilam Balam of Maní.* Norman: University of Oklahoma Press, 1979.

Edmonson, Munro S., trans. *The Ancient Future of the Itza: The Book of Chilam Balam of Tizimin*. Austin: University of Texas Press, 1982.

Elswit, Sharon Barcan. *The Latin American Story Finder: A Guide to 470 Tales from Mexico, Central America and South America, Listing Subjects and Sources*. Jefferson: McFarland & Company, Inc., 2015.

Ferguson, Diana. *Tales of the Plumed Serpent: Aztec, Inca and Maya Myths*. London: Collins & Brown, Ltd., 2000.

Goetz, Delia, and Sylvanus Griswold Morley. *Popol Vuh: The Book of the Ancient Maya*. Mineola: Dover Publications, 2003.

Green, Lila, ed. *Tales From Hispanic Lands*. Morristown: Silver Burdett Company, 1979.

Knowlton, Timothy, and Anthony Aveni. *Maya Creation Myths: Words and Worlds of the Chilam Balam.* Boulder: The University Press of Colorado, 2010.

Markman, Roberta H. and Peter T. Markman. *The Flayed God: The Mesoamerican Mythological Tradition*. New York: Harper Collins Publishers, 1992.

Menchú, Rigoberta, with Dante Liano. *The Honey Jar.* David Unger, trans. Berkeley: Groundwood Books, 2006.

Milbrath, Susan. *Star Gods of the Maya: Astronomy in Art, Folklore, and Calendars.* Austin: University of Texas Press, 1999.

Miller, Mary, and Karl Taube. *An Illustrated Dictionary of the Gods and Symbols of Ancient Mexico and the Maya.* London: Thames & Hudson, Ltd, 1993.

Nelson, Ralph, trans. *Popol Vuh: The Great Mythological Book of the Ancient Maya.* Boston: Houghton Mifflin Company, 1976.

Rice, Prudence M. *Maya Calendar Origins: Monuments, Myth History, and the Materialization of Time*. Austin: University of Texas Press, 2007.

Roberts, Timothy R. *Myths of the World: Gods of the Maya, Aztecs, and Incas*. New York: MetroBooks, 1996.

Roys, Ralph L. *The Book of Chilam Balam of Chumayel*. New ed. Norman: University of Oklahoma Press, 1967.

Sawyer-Lauçann, Christopher, trans. *The Destruction of the Jaguar: Poems from the Books of Chilam Balam*. San Francisco: City Lights Books, 1987.

Schmitt, Martha. *World Myths and Legends II: Central America*. Belmont: Simon & Schuster Education Group, 1993.

Schuman, Michael A. *Maya and Aztec Mythology*. Berkeley Heights: Enslow Publishers, Inc., 2001.

Sexton, James D., trans. and ed. *Mayan Folktales: Folklore from Lake Atitlan, Guatemala*. New York: Doubleday, 1992.

Taube, Karl. *The Legendary Past: Aztec and Maya Myths*. London: British Museum Press, 1993.

# Free Bonus from Captivating History (Available for a Limited time)

Hi History Lovers!

Now you have a chance to join our exclusive history list so you can get your first history ebook for free as well as discounts and a potential to get more history books for free! Simply visit the link below to join.

Captivatinghistory.com/ebook

Also, make sure to follow us on:

Twitter: @Captivhistory

Facebook: Captivating History:@captivatinghistory

Made in the USA
Middletown, DE
09 December 2022

17557708R00061